MASERATI 450S

A Bazooka from Modena

MASERATI 450S

Published 2023

ISBN: 978-1-956309-12-6

This book contains chassis histories based on publicly available information, as well as interviews and discussion with some of the recent or current car owners, their representatives and other marque experts.

Printed and bound at Interpress Ltd., Hungary

Dalton Watson Fine Books
Glyn and Jean Morris
Deerfield, IL 60015 USA

www.daltonwatson.com

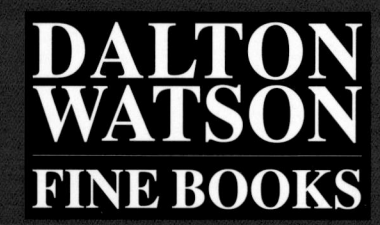

PREFACE

The 450S represents glorious triumph and tragic downfall like no other Maserati race car from the 1950s. It was the fastest front-engine race car of its time and if everything worked and when well maintained, the car was almost unbeatable in the hands of good drivers with superior skills to handle the beast.

In 1957, with just four races in Europe in just one year, the 450S gained a reputation as an incredibly fast car, but it had an enduring reputation for being unreliable. This was only in a few cases due to the car itself, but to the rather superficial preparation in the factory or by the mechanics on site. The car became a giant and a failure at the same time. As a result, the easier to drive and less powerful 300S, which was also used in Europe for several years, became a racing car icon and not the 450S.

But while all other easier-to-drive Maserati race cars have been involved in a few fatal accidents at some point, the 450S was spared. Due to its incredible power and the very high price Maserati asked for the car, it was not suited for the typical amateur race driver.

Following the tragic crash of Alfonso de Portago and Ed Nelson in the Ferrari 335S in the Mille Miglia that killed both drivers and nine spectators, over-powered cars like the 450S and its direct rivals from Ferrari, the 335S and 315S were banned by the F.I.A. in the World Sportscar Championship from 1958 on. As a result, all these cars remaining at both companies were sold to private owners in the United States, where they successfully continued their careers as the fastest front-engined racing cars in that period with such great drivers as Carroll Shelby, Bill Krause, Lloyd Ruby, Masten Gregory, Jim Hall and Chuck Daigh.

Walter Bäumer and Jean-François Blachette
December 2023

CONTENTS

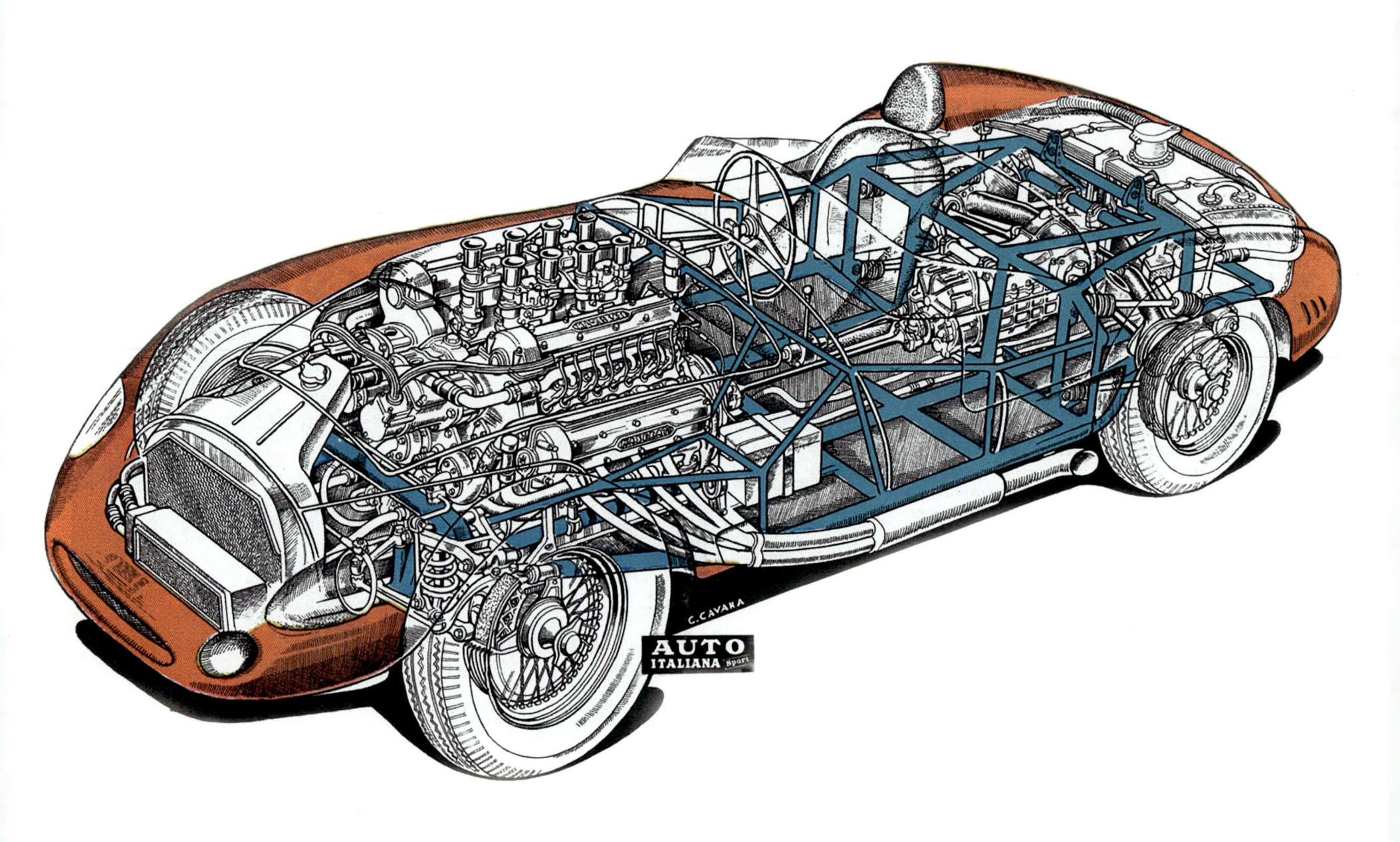

The Italian car magazine *Auto Italiana* used a Giovanni Cavara drawing of the 450S in 1957 and colored its chassis. *(Auto Italiana)*

TECHNICAL DEVELOPMENT

As early as 1954, Maserati was aware that the 300S would not remain competitive in the FIA World Sportscar Championship against the powerful Ferraris with their V12 engines.

Engineer Giulio Alfieri moved away from the typical Maserati 6-cylinder in-line engines and entrusted Engineer Guido Taddeucci, head of engine design, to develop a powerful V8 motor with four camshafts and dual ignition. The project had a code name, Tipo 54. It was the first V8 engine since the mid-1930s.

The initial development of the new alloy engine began with a 4,477-cc short-stroke V8 with 400 hp and four 45 IDM Weber carburetors mounted between the two-cylinder banks, with a bore x stroke of 93.8mm x 81mm, at 90° and double overhead camshafts rated at 400 hp at 7,200 rpm.

After the Le Mans tragedy in 1955 and due to other commitments in Maserati's racing program, the development of the motor stalled. In 1956, American car and race fanatic Tony Parravano from California visited Italy and commissioned Maserati to build a new large-bore V8 engine for use in a Kurtis Indy chassis. This made Maserati resume working on the Tipo 54 project once again. The first prototype engine was installed into a 350S chassis and transported to Sweden for the Grand Prix in 1956 where all drivers tested the car in practice. None of them was convinced by it and complained about the vibrations which came from a firing order that was also used by other manufacturers (see the #4501 chapter).

With a new crankshaft and camshafts, this vibrating was finally eliminated, and, on the dyno, the power output was 412 hp at 7,000 rpm. Respected journalist, Denis Jenkinson, wrote in *Motor Sport*: "...[the 450S] is known affectionately by all at Maserati, and most of Modena, as the 'quattro mezzo' and the sound of its thunderous exhaust note as it is run on the testbed causes most of Modena to give knowing smiles…"

This enormous power, defined by many as monstrous, caused driving problems which required great sensitivity by the drivers in working the accelerator. Moss later wrote in one of his books, that it was not easy to start the 450S. Denis Jenkinson: "...Getaway from standstill on a high bottom gear, with a rather fierce clutch, is anything but easy and is rather slow but once the clutch is home and the revs build up black lines appear on the road behind the rear wheels [...] Even with this sort of standing start it is possible to do 0-100mph in an easy 11 sec., but the real surge of acceleration is in the 80mph to 170mph range"

The chassis of the 450S corresponded to the usual tubular frame chassis that all racing cars used at the time. Maserati was known for its chassis, which enabled very balanced handling in the smaller types such as the 150S, 200S and A6GCS. The frame of the 450S was an extended version of the 300S chassis but with a completely redesigned rear layout. It is worth noting, that the development of more powerful engines was ahead of the chassis design that was still based on earlier general principles. Maserati worked on the chassis of the later cars, probably from #4504 on, and mounted double shock absorbers since the Houdailles tended to break at the lever attachments.

The big 5-speed gearbox, designed by Valerio Colotti, had its shafts in line with the axis of the car. The tube of the de Dion rear axle ran across the chassis behind the axle and was located by a guide fixed to the chassis frame. Rear suspension came with a high-mounted transverse leaf spring and twin-radius rods located near the rear axle assembly. To house all these components, the chassis was much tougher but also heavier than the chassis used in the smaller 300S. This huge gearbox became the Achilles' heel of the 450S and eventually caused problems in all the cars.

In preparation for the Mille Miglia in 1957, the car for Moss, #4505, was equipped with an additional two-speed gearbox inserted between the engine and the transmission and its purpose was to enable the driver to select either a set of high ratios or a set of low ratios. It worked like on overdrive and turned out to be very effective (see the #4505 chapter).

After his ingenious bodywork for the 300S, Medardo Fantuzzi was also entrusted with the production of the new coachwork for the 450S. The prototype engine was installed in the unlucky 350S car he had designed and arrived for the 1956 Swedish Grand Prix with a huge bulge on the front hood to cover the upright carburetor pipes.

Maserati technician and later archivist Ermanno Cozza wrote about this enormous bulge in his book Maserati at Heart: "... [Engineer] Reggiani subsequently had the idea of inclining the carburetors towards the inside with new intake manifolds, searching for a carburetion compromise that would permit shorter intake trumpets. With this configuration the engine and carburetor assembly were much lower, making the bulge on the bonnet much more attractive and improving visibility for the driver."

Fantuzzi's design for the 450S was finally again an attractive body that clearly followed the visual concept of the 300S, just in larger dimensions. From #4507 on the coachwork became a little beefier in the overall lines.

Testing of the car was either done on the Aerautodromo in the center of Modena or on open roads around the city. Maserati team driver Jean Behra tried the 450S several times on the road to Maranello, driving ol' Enzo crazy when he heard the powerful noise of the car. Behra wrecked a 450S on such a test drive on an open road just prior to the 1957 Mille Miglia and landed in hospital (see the #4503 chapter).

In total Maserati developed four different versions of the 450S engine: Tipo 54 with 4,543cc and 400hp which was the prototype motor. The next was the 4,477cc version with 400hp which became the standard version for the 450S. Then an engine with 4,680 cc for #4508 only. The fourth version was for Indianapolis with 4,190cc and 395 hp. The type 59 with 5,665cc which came out with 520 hp at 7,000 rpm, used with success in two cars. In the meantime, Maserati had developed the 450S engine in marine version, equally dominating as it had been more briefly in the automobile field, the type 62 with 6,462cc developing the enormous power of 580hp. Complete with a gear reduction unit built by Maserati, these units weighed 390kg.

The chassis including suspension and with its engine and gearbox fitted. This photograph was taken in December 1956, so it is most likely chassis #4504. *(Bernard Cahier Archives)*

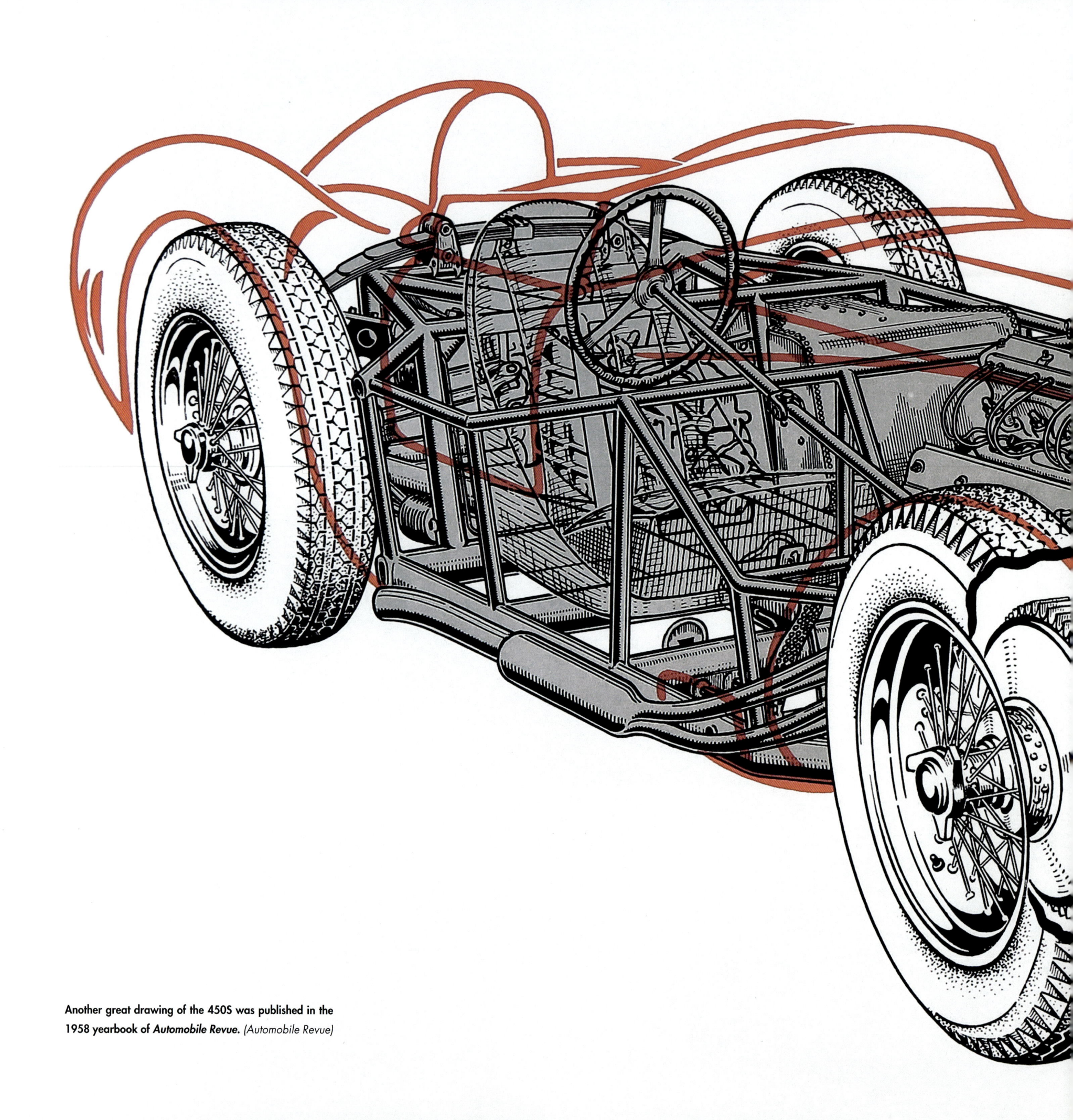

Another great drawing of the 450S was published in the
1958 yearbook of *Automobile Revue.* (Automobile Revue)

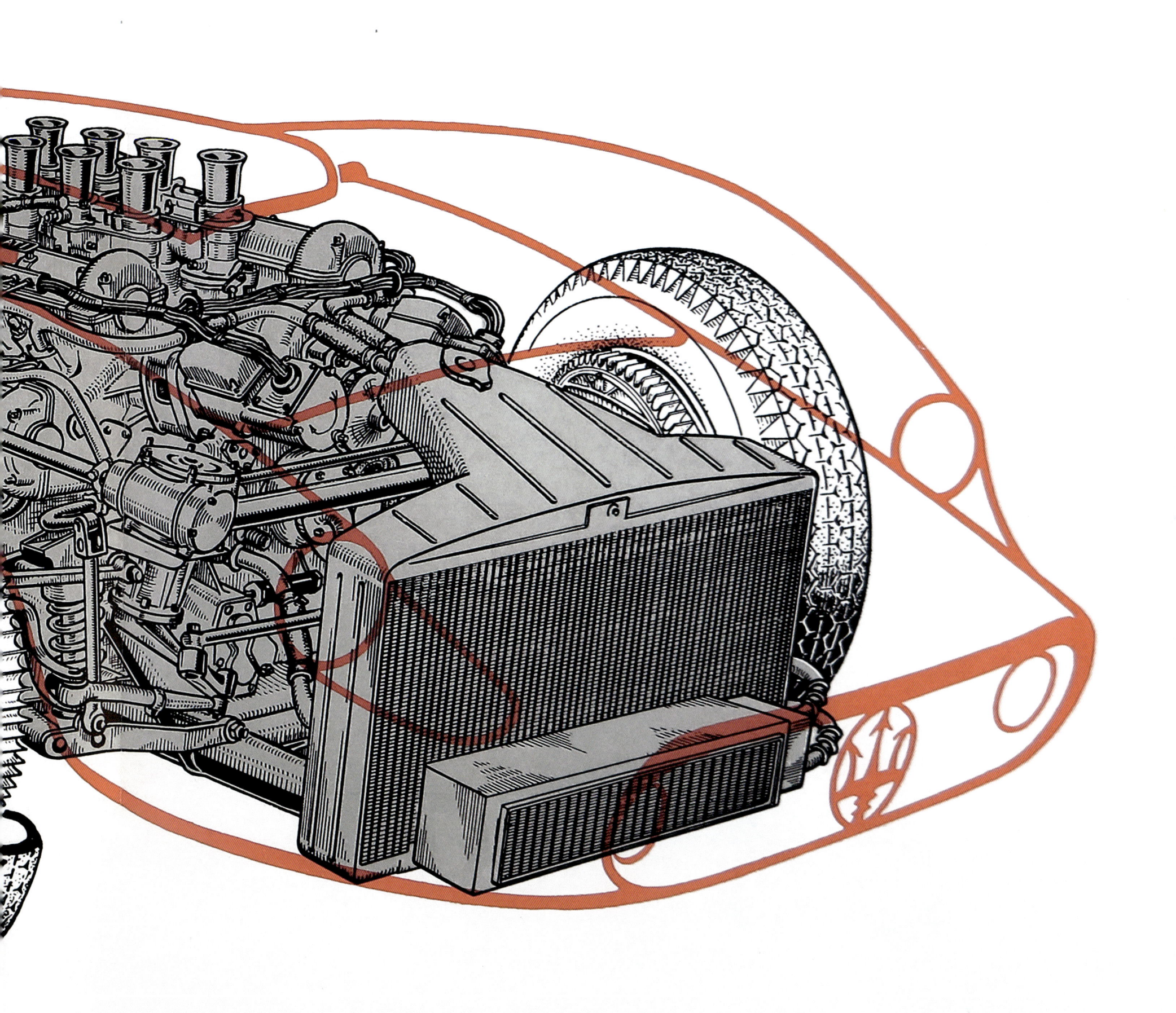

Technical Data

Steering:	worm and sector
Length:	4,350 mm (171.3")
Width:	1,550 mm (61")
Height:	1,000 mm (39.4")
Wheelbase:	2,400 mm (94.5")
Track (fr/r):	1,333 mm (52.5")/1,298 mm (51.1")
Wheels (fr/r):	5 x 16/5.5 x 16
Tyres (fr/r):	6 x 16/7 x 16
Dry weight	790kg
	1180kg for the Zagato Coupé
Fuel tank:	140 lt

Acceleration (km/h)

0-30 km/h (s):	1.3
0-40 km/h (s):	1.6
0-50 km/h (s):	2
0-60 km/h (s):	2.3
0-70 km/h (s):	2.6
0-80 km/h (s):	3
0-90 km/h (s):	3.3
0-100 km/h (s):	3.7
0-110 km/h (s)	4.7
0-120 km/h (s):	5.3
0-130 km/h (s):	5.9
0-140 km/h (s):	6.5
0-150 km/h (s):	7.2
0-160 km/h (s):	7.9
0-170 km/h (s):	8.8
0-180 km/h (s):	10.3
0-190 km/h (s):	11.3
0-200 km/h (s):	12.5
0-210 km/h (s):	13.9
0-220 km/h (s):	16
0-230 km/h (s):	17.8
0-240 km/h (s):	20.3
0-250 km/h (s):	23.6
0-270 km/h (s):	33.4

Acceleration (mp/h)

0-20 mph (s):	1.3
0-30 mph (s):	1.9
0-40 mph (s):	2.5
0-50 mph (s):	3
0-60 mph (s):	3.5
0-70 mph (s):	4.9
0-80 mph (s):	5.8
0-90 mph (s):	6.8
0-100 mph (s):	8
0-110 mph (s):	9.8
0-120 mph (s):	11.7
0-130 mph (s):	13.8
0-140 mph (s):	16.9
0-150 mph (s):	20.7
0-160 mph (s):	27.3
0-180 mph (s):	not measured
0-200 mph (s):	not measured

Overtaking factors (through gears)

60-100 km/h (sec):	1.4
80-120 km/h (sec):	2.3
100-180 km/h (sec):	6.6
40-70 mph (sec):	2.4
50-90 mph (sec):	not measured

Speed range (km/h/mph)

(max speed on gears, top gear value theor.)

(km/h/mph)

I:	105/65
II:	174/108
III:	219/136
IV:	244/152
V:	306/190

1000rpm speed: (km/h/mph)

I:	14/8.7
II:	23.2/14.4
III:	29.2/18.1
IV:	32.6/20.3
V:	40.8/25.4

The massive bell housing for the 5-speed gearbox and a drive shaft. In the back are some cylinder heads for the 450S. *(Zagari/Spitzley Archive)*

OPPOSITE: The front suspension and heavily finned drum brake of the 450S. Maserati was famous for its beautifully designed components. *(Zagari / Spitzley Archive)*

Chassis #4503 was returned from the successful race in Sebring in 1957 to the factory to be refreshed and modified. *(Klemantaski Collection)*

The mounted gearbox in the rear part of the chassis. *(Bernard Cahier Archives)*

The big engine requested a massive
water cooler. *(Klemantaski Collection)*

Mechanics Giulio Borsari and Antonio Reggiani working on a 450S engine when mounted on the dyno. After Maserati withdrew from racing, Borsari worked for Scuderia Centro Sud and later for the Ferrari F1-team. *(Walter Bäumer Collection)*

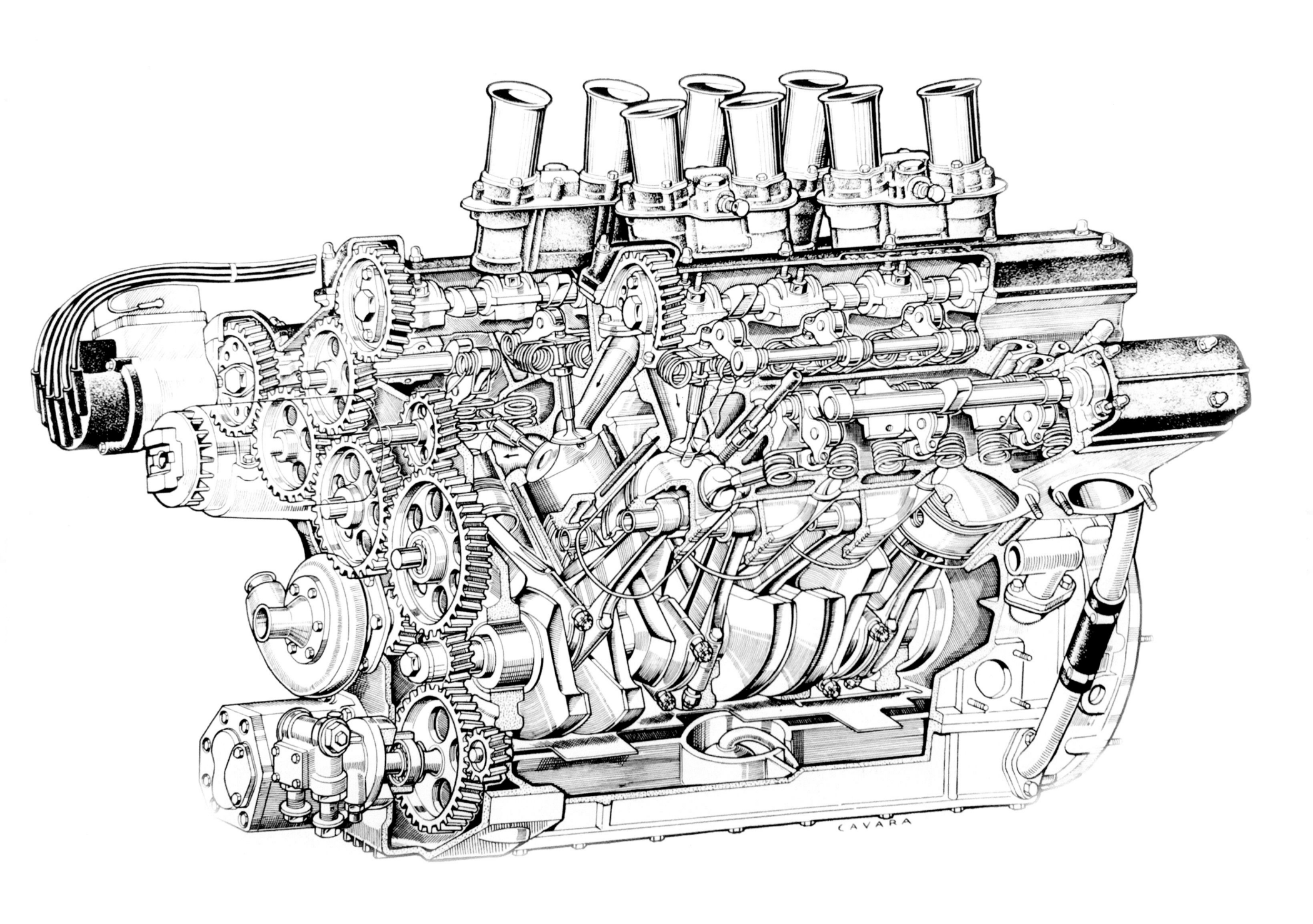

A cutaway drawing of the mighty 450S engine. The gear drive of the four camshafts are clearly visible. *(Cavara)*

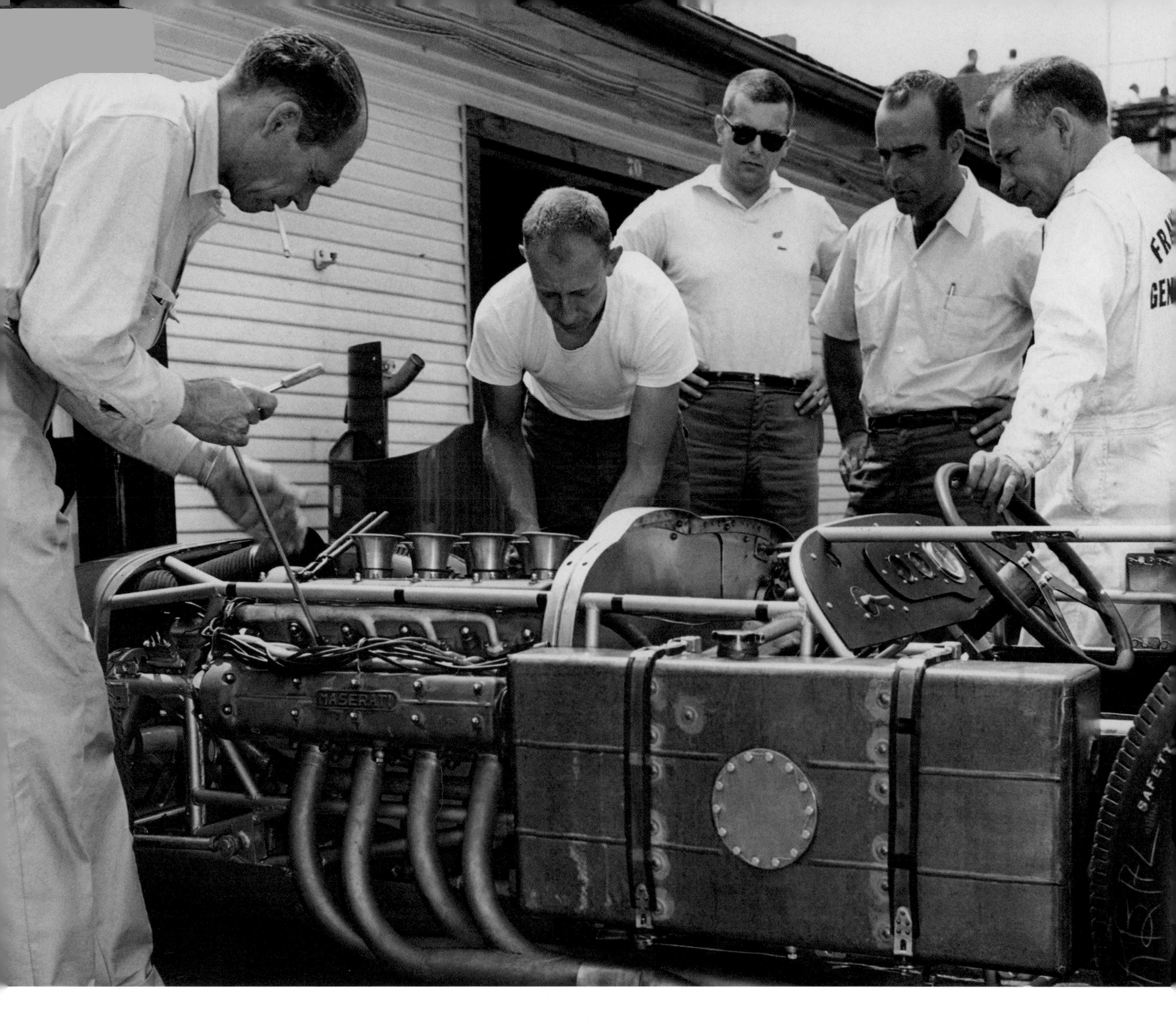

OPPOSITE: Jean Behra tested chassis #4503 in Monza on March 24, 1957. *(Walter Bäumer Collection)*

One of the 450S spare engines Tony Parravano had bought from the factory ended up in the Arciero-owned Kurtis/Maserati for the Indianapolis 500 in May 1959. *(Walter Bäumer Collection)*

MASERATI SPORT 450/S

PROMOTION & SALES

Until the very late 1950s, Maserati was never good in promoting their cars. They promoted their 2-liter A6GCS with an individual sales brochure as the main clientele was the ambitious amateur racer, mainly in Italy and the company sold no less than 53 cars, mainly in Europe.

Because the powerful 450S was not easy to drive and served as a factory tool for experienced drivers like Fangio, Moss and Behra and was not intended purely as a customer car and incredibly expensive for the time. Because of this, Maserati S.p.A. saw no need to invest money in any expanded promotional activities.

Maserati only produced two sales sheets for the type as they did that for the previous very successful 300S. The first version of the 450S sheets shows chassis number #4502 with the short exhaust pipes coming out of both sides of the

coachwork and the second version most likely shows chassis number #4505 or #4507. Both versions show the same technical data on the reverse of this sales sheet. In Europe, too, the car was not advertised in car newspapers and magazines and not a single 450S was sold on that continent.

Only the Italian car magazine *Auto Italiana* reported extensively on the new car but only in one of their issues from early 1957.

Maserati Corporation of America (MCA), the official Maserati importer for the USA in Long Island, New York, only briefly promoted the new V8 in their March 1957 newsletter *MCA Racing News* with a small photo of chassis number #4502 but reported in detail about the victory of Fangio and Behra in the new type in Sebring 1957. The car was incredibly expensive for the time, even by American standards and so Frank Harrison the owner of the last car made, chassis #4510, had to transfer US$16,180 to Modena. But it is doubtful whether the 450S paid off financially for Maserati S.p.A.

MASERATI SPORT 450/S

MASERATI SPORT 450/S

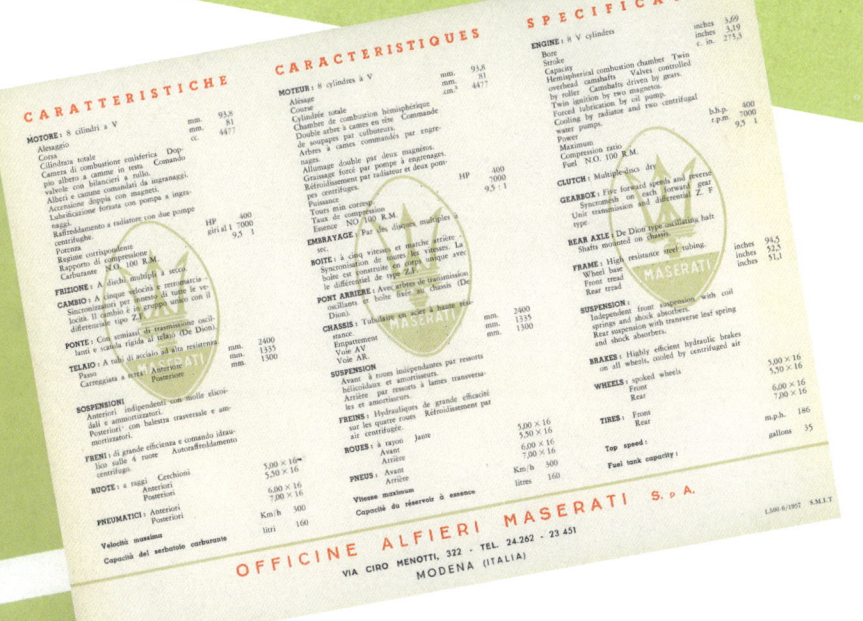

A fantastic shot of chassis #4505 with Moss passing the grandstand on the straight of the Nürburgring in 1957 for the 1,000 km race. A little later the car became a "Three-Wheeler". *(Klemantaski Collection)*

THE COMPETITION

THE WORLD SPORTSCAR CHAMPIONSHIP

The community of motor sport enthusiasts today regards the 1950s as the Golden Age. Big advertising stickers on cars were not common, no public relations campaigns were launched, and all the VIP brouhaha seen today was almost non-existent. Some of the important manufacturers of the time such as Ferrari, Maserati, Mercedes-Benz, Gordini and Lancia produced single-seater racing cars to compete in the Formula 1 World Championship which was established in 1950. But they also, with the exception of Mercedes-Benz, had their eyes on the private wealthy amateur racer for whom they made sports racing cars to enter in the various street races and hill climbs. Jaguar, Aston Martin, Porsche and many more were also in this category.

After the International Sporting Commission (CSI) of the Paris-based Federation International de l'Automobile (FIA) announced the World Sportscar Championship in 1953 this series became the most important venue for all the great marques. All cars had to comply with Appendix C of its regulations, requiring two seats, full lighting equipment, rear-view mirrors, an inflated spare wheel, horn, two doors, self-starter and later, for the 1957 edition, a windshield wiper, and for open cars, the ability to fit a hood over the cockpit. In most cases this latter requirement resulted in some very strange temporary contraptions and was not very practical. A point system was set, awarding eight points for the winner, six for second place, four for third place, three for the car in fourth, two for fifth and one for sixth. The aggregate of a car's four best performances in seven races would decide the new champion and the winner would receive the Manufacturers' Cup.

The World Sportscar Championship (WSCC) became the battlefield for Mercedes-Benz, Jaguar, Lancia, Ferrari, Aston Martin, Porsche, OSCA and Maserati and their participation gave this series its glamour and worldwide attention. Held on public roads of sometimes questionable quality, like the legendary Mille Miglia, in the terrible heat of Buenos Aires, on daunting circuits like the Nürburgring, the high-speed flat of the Sebring airfield, and the day and night of the 24 Hours of Le Mans, the series was always a challenge to men and machine, taking both to their limits.

Maserati had its new weapon, the 450S, fitted with a 4.5-liter V8 engine with four camshafts and 400hp. It was the fastest sports racing car of the 1950s and the roar of the engine on the factory test bench could be heard all over Modena. Together with the improved 300S, it gave high hopes for revenge for the disappointment of 1956.

New regulations were announced by the FIA in a revised Appendix C. The "prototype" clause, which had restricted engines to a 2.5-liter capacity in 1956, was relaxed which left the door open for much bigger sports cars. However, the cars were required to have two doors, a full-width windscreen of minimum dimension of 100cm wide by 15cm high, and provision for the fitting of a soft-top "roof."

The maiden entry for the 450S in a WSCC event came on August 12, 1956, when the factory arrived in Sweden with the prototype (see the #3501/4501

chapter). It was a rather dull car, and all Maserati team drivers tested it but had no positive opinion about it.

For the first round of the 1957 Championship, the team appeared in Buenos Aires in Argentina for the 1,000 km race in January. The organizers had switched circuits to a long counter straight that most drivers found very dangerous. Over the winter, Maserati had developed the 450S to be a serious contender and driven by Fangio, Behra and Moss, its big V8 showed its full potential and dominance over the Ferraris, who protested the speed of the Maserati and in response, the organizers built a chicane or additional curve overnight to slow the cars down. But there was more trouble, for the Argentine Automobile Club declared that it had received the new FIA rules too late in November of the previous year and so the owners had insufficient time to modify their cars to the new standards. The organization did not want to compromise and so the cars in question were required either to be modified or withdrawn from the event. More difficulties occurred when the starting procedure was changed overnight to a mass start with engines running, but finally there was the "Go!" and 26 cars were on their way.

Maserati had four official cars on the grid: the 450S driven by Fangio and Moss, a 350S for local driver Roberto Bonomi with Italian Luigi Piotti, and two 300S. The Milan-based Scuderia Madunina had entered a private 300S for Oscar Cabalen and Carlo Tomasi. American Masten Gregory was with Eugenio Castellotti in a Ferrari 290 MM while Alfonso de Portago and Peter Collins had a second car, and two more team cars of the same type were driven by Wolfgang von Trips with Luigi Musso and the friends Collins and Mike Hawthorn.

In the race, Moss drove the 450S to an early lead over thirty-three laps when Fangio took over and cranked out an incredible lap at 106 mph. It was here that the 450S received its nickname, "Bazooka." The car was so fast that nobody could keep up. Only Gregory made good progress until he turned over the 290 MM to Castellotti. Then, what Cyril Posthumus describes in his fantastic book about the WSCC as "the old game of motor racing musical chairs," began again: Musso took over the car from Castellotti and gave it to von Trips. De Portago turned his car over to Musso but was replaced by Collins as his own car was out of order after only three laps. It seemed it would be a Maserati win when Fangio returned to the pits on the fifty-seventh lap with no clutch. A withdrawal pin had fallen out causing a broken crown wheel. The fastest car was out.

But the 12 Hours of Sebring with Fangio and Behra behind the wheel about one month later, astonished the entire opposition with the speed of the car. Crossing the finish line as the winner gave Maserati one of the biggest glory days in its history.

After the start, Collins drove his Ferrari into the lead for the first twenty-five laps but Behra in the 450S closed in, passing him with ease. Then Fangio took over the driving and increased the lead by some ten miles over the Ferrari driven by Musso and de Portago. Unfortunately, Guerino Bertocchi, Maserati's chief mechanic mistakenly ordered a premature refueling for the 300S driven by Shelby and Salvadori and the car was disqualified, but the first 300S with Moss and Schell

The racetrack at the 1,000 km race in Buenos Aires shocked all drivers as there was direct oncoming traffic on a long straight without any safety separation. *(Walter Bäumer Collection)*

Drivers getting ready for the Le Mans start for the 12 Hours of Sebring in 1957. Note the cardboard covers attached with adhesive tape to the headlights to protect them against stone chips. A third lamp is mounted on the lower lip of the radiator opening. *(Walter Bäumer Collection)*

Before the start of the Mille Miglia 1957, Maserati chief mechanic Guerino Bertocchi fiddles with the strange top link that the FIA requested for every car in the World Sportscar Championship from 1957 onwards. *(Walter Bäumer Collection)*

OPPOSITE: The start of the 1,000 km race on the Nürburgring in 1957. Both 450S (no. 1 and 2) failed to finish. The happy winner became the Aston Martin DBR1 (no. 14). *(Klemantaski Collection)*

gave a wonderful performance. The Ferraris began having brake problems, disastrous on a circuit such as Sebring which required perfect brake balance. In the meantime, the Jaguar of Hawthorn and Bueb had managed to overtake the Musso/ de Portago car and was in second place. By now Moss was driving in the way only Moss could, pushing his 300S into the leading group. With one hour to go the Jaguar had a three-minute lead over the Maseratis but was having brake problems as well. Moss placed second while the 450S of Fangio, still in the lead, lapped the Jaguar for the fifth time, and won the race, with Moss holding on to second.

It was a great day for Officine Maserati. The Ferraris were not so lucky. Hill had to retire his car and those of Collins/Trintignant and Musso/de Portago arrived in sixth and seventh place respectively. The privately-entered Ferrari of Gregory and Brero took fourth place. Maserati was leading the World Sportscar Championship for the first time! Entering the Mille Miglia was a question of

OPPOSITE: Harry Schell had just jumped behind the wheel in #4503 to start the 1,000 km race on the Nürburgring. Moss is next to him in #4505. Both cars did not see the finish and the happy winner became the Aston Martin DBR1. *(Walter Bäumer Collection)*

Harry Schell with chassis #4503 was fastest starter in the 1,000 km Nürburgring while #4505 had difficulties moving on. This race attracted over 100,000 spectators each year. *(Unknown photographer)*

honor for both Maserati and Ferrari, but the Mille Miglia in May 1957 became a disaster for Maserati (see the #4505 chapter). Moss and his co-driver and journalist Denis Jenkinson were pushed in the car back to Brescia after only a few miles when the brake pedal fell off. After the triumph in Sebring, frustration returned to Maserati. The Mille Miglia became the race of the Ferraris. Collins with photographer Klemantaski on board was on his way to win but had to stop only eighty miles from the finish when the differential of his Ferrari 315S with a 4.1-liter engine broke.

Taruffi, the man of pre- and postwar fame, drove alone and was in the race of his life in an identical car. It was his fourteenth attempt to win this race, and he finally triumphed, after being caught and briefly overtaken near Mantua by von Trips in his 3.8-liter Ferrari 335S. Von Trips came in second, and Olivier Gendebien was third with his Ferrari 250 TDF co-driven by Jacques Washer. Only 25 minutes later the Maserati 300S of Scarlatti appeared in Brescia taking fourth place. It was one of Maserati's best finishes ever in the Mille Miglia. Then the shocking news arrived: Alfonso de Portago had crashed near Guidizzolo when the left front tire of his 335S was punctured and the car went off the road, killing him, his co-driver Eddie Nelson and eleven spectators instantly. This tragedy spoilt Ferrari's triumph, and the Italian Government soon after banned motor racing on public roads. Ferrari's tragic success gave them the needed points to be back in the game, and they were now leading Maserati by two points in the Championship.

The next event was on May 26 at the Nürburgring 1,000 km. The big surprise was the Aston Martin team from England which had brought two of its new DBR1 cars to the Eifel Mountains. Maserati entered two of its V8 cars, two 300S and a 350S on the difficult circuit and was confident of repeating the success of the year before. The 350S was only there for testing and confirmed that Maserati had no real confidence in the further development of the 300S. Ferrari had its strong 335S, a 315S, and the prototype of its forthcoming Testa Rossa on the grid, next to three Jaguar D-Types and an armada of Porsches.

Behra was still handicapped by his pre-Mille Miglia accident and so Fangio, who had only a contract for Formula 1 events with Maserati, agreed to save Trident honor. He was assigned to drive the V8 and in practice turned in a remarkable 9:43.5 min. lap, but Moss in the second V8 was slower than Tony Brooks in his DBR1. The Aston Martin led the race for the first eight laps until Moss caught him and was then leading for two laps until he retired with a broken half shaft. Fangio was passed by the Ferraris and Moss took over the car after a long pit stop only to retire after one more lap. So it was, again, the job of the 300S to save Maserati honor. Ugolini signaled Bonnier and Scarlatti to the pits and Moss took over their car, but after one lap returned with rear suspension problems. Francisco Godia-Sales was driving his own 300S as a factory entry. His co-driver Horace Gould was ordered in, and Moss jumped into his fourth Maserati. Moss pushed the car from eleventh to sixth place, and then Fangio took over and made it up to fifth. But it was left to Brooks to pick up the laurels, giving the victory to the much smaller Aston Martin. About four minutes behind was the Ferrari of Collins and Gendebien, and Hawthorn/Trintignant were third. This result gave Ferrari 25 points in the Championship over the 19 points Maserati had to its credit.

The 24 Hours of Le Mans was back on the agenda of the WSCC this year, and Maserati once again hoped for success with the 450S for speed was essential on the Sarthe circuit. One of these cars had been converted to a coupé by Zagato, based on the ideas of Frank Costin, the Lotus aerodynamicist. But Zagato's interpretation of the design was not entirely satisfactory, and it was soon clear to Moss, who tried the car in practice, that this "bastard" would not do anything for him. It turned out to be slower than the open car and was unpleasant for the drivers for the cockpit reached very high temperatures.

Behra and fellow Frenchman André Simon were assigned to a second 450S. The race was a disaster for Maserati as Moss had to retire his troubled car after a little more than two hours, and the open V8 of Behra/Simon was stranded at Mulsanne corner after twenty-eight laps. Scarlatti and Bonnier drove an upgraded early 300S, #3056, but the car failed on the seventy-third lap with clutch problems. Once again, the Maserati cars demonstrated their apparent dislike of the French long-distance race, which was won this time by a Jaguar D-Type driven by Bueb and Flockhart with three more D-Types taking the next places. The best Ferrari was in fifth place, being the 315S of Stuart Lewis-Evans and Martino Severi. Ferrari had now a comfortable lead with 27 points and Maserati was struggling with 19 points.

The Grand Prix of Sweden, which had replaced the Dundrod event, would be decisive for both Italian teams and so two 450S and one 300S arrived from Modena, along with two 335S and two 250 Testa Rossa from Ferrari, plus several private cars with the Maranello badge. The brutish power of the 450S gave Moss the lead over Hawthorn in his Ferrari after six laps. Behra in the second V8 passed Hill on lap ten and Hawthorn on lap fifteen. The Frenchman was unstoppable, and he even outpaced Moss after seventeen laps to take the lead. Behra bettered the lap record of Fangio no less than three times, and both 450S were superior to all the Ferraris. Moss stopped, handed over the car to Schell, to take over Behra's car, but soon Schell had to retire the car with transmission failure. Ugolini once more acted and stopped the 300S with Scarlatti for Schell to take over. Moss returned with the V8 and Behra resumed driving while Moss replaced Schell in the 300S. The Ferrari driven by Hawthorn and Musso had constant problems during the race. Behra finished first, Hill and Collins came back in second, and Moss again performed miracles, pushing his beloved 300S into third place. Thanks to Moss, the situation for Maserati improved. Maserati was now had 25 points behind its Modenese archrival Ferrari with 28 points. The last chance for Maserati to become the champions was the seventh and final round, far away on the Caracas, Venezuela circuit. What has not been written about this dramatic Grand Prix of Venezuela on the street circuit in Caracas on November 3, 1957? The World Sportscar Championship was at the peak of excitement. The announced prize money was large and was topped by a solid gold cup which President Marcos Jimenez had for the winner.

But race preparations in Caracas became chaotic for Maserati and Fangio. The ex-Argentinian dictator Juan Perón, who was in exile in Venezuela, indirectly precipitated the first crisis. The political relationship between the Venezuelan and post-Peron Argentinian regimes was very difficult since Venezuela was sheltering Peron and the upshot was that Fangio, an Argentine citizen, and Maserati's

Two Maserati 450S entered by the factory sitting side by side during refueling before the first practice session at 1957 Le Mans. *(Bernard Cahier Archives)*

number one driver, who had been assigned by Hans Tanner to the big 450S owned by Temple Buell, could not get permission to race in Caracas. Tanner was able to replace Fangio with Dale Duncan, a relative of team member Masten Gregory, who flew in from Kansas.

Then, before the race, Giambertone and Tanner had a difficult time extricating the racing cars from Venezuelan customs at the La Guaira seaport. Next, there was no transporter available to take the cars to the circuit so they would have to be driven. No local license plates were available, and those from Italy could not be used on the superhighway between La Guaira and Caracas and Giambertone and his crew could not see driving $45,000 worth of highly-strung racing machinery over donkey trails. Someone finally obtained a set of President Jimenez's personal license plates for them to use.

Hans Tanner later reported to an unknown magazine: "...In the midst of all this, Stirling Moss and Tony Brooks announced their refusal to drive. Their passports had been lifted and they weren't going to budge until they got them back. Then Ugolini brought the news that the tires that had been shipped from America were being held up – some law that prohibits importing any tire of a size already being manufactured in Venezuela. Without the tires, we had less than half the rubber we were going to need for six hundred miles at almost a hundred miles an hour ... for four cars.

"...Colonel Morro of the Venezuelan Auto Club recovered the passports for Moss and Brooks and the Firestone agency in Caracas managed to sort out the tire problem. Then came a big blow for Nello Ugolini. He received a cable saying that his father was very ill and not expected to live. He immediately placed a call to Italy, but it was too late, for his father had already died. Ugolini went to pieces and the entire Maserati team was torn by their sympathy for him and the need for him as team manager the next morning..."

More than one hundred thousand spectators were next to the road circuit or sitting on the walls high above. This 6.2-mile circuit was wide and fast but also had a slow hairpin that was badly marked. When the drivers had a first view of the circuit, they were horrified. The course was formed out of the public road system leading into Caracas and made use of a flyover to connect two sides of a dual highway. The marking of the roads was extremely poor as a shocked Phil Hill found when he drove five miles down one road flat-out during practice and met traffic coming against him. After the drivers complained about the dangerous

The start in Caracas 1957. Mike Hawthorn in his Ferrari 335S (no. 12) had the best start. Masten Gregory in chassis #4508 was ahead of all the Maseratis, while Moss in #4507 (no. 4) and Behra in #4503 (no. 2) are still standing. The beginning of the drama... *(Phil Hill Family Archive)*

conditions, some improvements were made overnight, and a chicane was set up on the circuit following complaints from Ferrari who found the big 450S too fast in practice. There was a nervous atmosphere, and everybody knew that this race would be the big showdown between Maserati and Ferrari, and that both teams had brought their best cars. Along with a pair of 450S Maseratis to be shared by Moss, Behra and Schell, a private 450S had been entered by Temple Buell with Gregory behind the wheel and also a single 300S to be driven by Bonnier. Englishman Tony Brooks, in his only drive in a Maserati, partnered Moss in his V8.

What happened on the day that changed Maserati history forever? In the first lap Gregory slowed down ahead of a tricky, dangerously narrow turn over a bridge and, pleased with himself, could not resist throwing a look over his shoulder to see how far behind he had left the Ferraris – and this was a big mistake! He crashed the car, rolled and came to a halt upside down, luckily crawling away with only minor injuries. Moss in his 450S settled down in the lead but on lap thirty-three he was driving at his customary 165mph, when an American, A.P. Dressel, swung his 2-liter A.C.-Bristol across his path. With some 65mph speed differential between the two cars… the impact was terrific. Moss very luckily being cast out, suffered only a severe shaking.

That left two works Maseratis. The plucky Moss walked back to the pits, arriving just in time to see Behra's car catch fire while refueling. The fire was extinguished but Behra and Bertocchi were slightly burnt. When Moss took the wheel, everybody presumed that the fire was extinguished. Six laps later, however, Moss came back. The fire was still smoldering under the driver's seat. Harry Schell took over the car.

Posthumus: "Schell was gaining rapidly …when he came up on the outside of Jo Bonnier's 300S. Both cars were doing over 120mph, when suddenly the rear tire burst on Bonnier's car, which lurched and skidded into Schell with appalling effect. The 3-liter cannoned across the read, smack into a concrete telegraph post, which broke and fell straight across the cockpit, bare seconds after Bonnier has leapt out. The 450S slammed against a wall, then bounced off, the fuel tank burst, and the car caught fire… Bonnier and Schell picked themselves up, one cut and bleeding, the other burned, both dazed with shock, but alive."

Some sources claim that Maserati race director Nello Ugolini had informed all his drivers before the start that all their cars had already been sold after the race and therefore every effort should be made by the drivers not to damage them. Each of the 450S had a value of almost US$10,000 and the 300S of US$8,000, money that was much needed, and the plan had been to sell the cars after the race, decorated with the expected laurels, to wealthy private drivers from South America. But the tragic result combined with the failure of the post-Peron government in Argentina to pay for a consignment of tools and machinery was all too much for the small car manufacturer. In January 1958, Omar Orsi, President of Officine Maserati, announced the official withdrawal of Maserati from motor racing.

RACING IN THE UNITED STATES

At the end of World War II in the late 1940s, many American GIs returned from Europe bringing with them examples of the small racing cars from the 1930s that they had seen whilst on active duty. In this way, countless Alfa Romeos, Mercedes, Bugattis, Delahayes, Jaguars, MGs, Lancias and others were imported into the US. Possibly because this kind of car did not previously exist in the US, they soon developed an enthusiastic following, particularly in California. The US economy was growing, and it was not long before the attention of wealthy car enthusiasts was focused on these exotic high-performance cars. People like Briggs Cunningham, John von Neumann and Jim Kimberly of Kimberly-Clark, the paper company, had enough money to buy these Italian exotics and run race operations all over the US. Later John Edgar and Tony Parravano, perhaps the most colorful of them all, bought their "toys" from Italy for drivers like Carroll Shelby, Masten Gregory, Phil Hill and Jack McAfee.

Life was fun for those who were heavily involved in the US racing scene in those days as can be seen from the many photographs, for example, of John Edgar's Ferrari race cars parked on the lawn next to his swimming pool or as he drove his 450S to the restaurant (see the #4506 chapter). Some of the races were surrounded by life-style facilities like golf, pool resorts, fishing lodges etc. and the main reason for the teams and drivers to go to Nassau in the British Bahamas was for "havin' a party and chasing girls."

Almost all the races within the US were organized under the banner of the Sports Car Club of America (SCCA) in close collaboration with the California Sports Car Club (CSCC) and the American Automobile Association (AAA). The SCCA was founded in the 1940s and was strictly devoted to the amateur status of its members, counting 9,000 in 1957. Public roads were used at first, but the outcry over the noise and inconvenience of closing the roads, as well as the safety issue, doomed this type of racing after several accidents occurred involving spectators. Unlike Europe where a major race would continue all day and include all classes of cars run over long distances, the SCCA races were constrained by the large turnout, sometimes as many as 200 to 300 cars, and the small tracks available. There was just no way to run 200 cars on a two-mile track all at the same time. The SCCA broke the entries up into groups of 20 similar cars and gave each group equal track time. This also kept cars with similar speed together. The results of a preliminary race were not aggregated with the results of the main race, a system called heat racing. The main or final class race held on Sunday, except in Connecticut where it was illegal to race on Sunday before 2 pm, was the one that would count for points and trophies. All other racing was just to give competitors more track time.

In 1951, Miles Collier and others tried to convince the SCCA to allow professional drivers to participate as well. This proposal encountered many political problems and disagreements between some of the drivers, the owners, and the SCCA. The race teams of Tony Parravano and John Edgar were more or less professional operations, and they all paid their drivers. Edgar's spectacular Pullman-type transporter attracted the crowds wherever it appeared. As the sport became bigger, the discussions became more and more heated. Members of the

Almost everything in the US is showtime and some of the flagmen could jump quite high to start the pack. Chassis #4506 and Dan Gurney are beside Fred Knoop's Huffaker/Chevy at Tracy in May 1958. *(Revs Institute)*

SCCA were dismissed whenever they participated with or against professional racers even if they did not accept prize money, and the situation became more absurd as drivers were allowed to make money abroad. Consequently, drivers like Shelby, Hill, and Gregory went to Europe to earn their fees and acquire the international reputation most US races could not offer.

In 1956, to attract overseas entries, the officials of the professional event, 12 Hours of Sebring, stated for the first time that there would be prize money of US$10,000 on top of the starting money. This was offered by Alec Ulmann who had virtually written the SCCA rules. But this did not heal the difficult rift between professional and amateur drivers. As other clubs which gave cash to their participants were founded, the SCCA and CSCC came under increased pressure but stayed strictly with their unrealistic rules until 1963. By that time the SCCA had nine areas with ninety-six regions under its banner.

As a result of this debate the United States Automobile Club (USAC), the FIA representative in the US, tried to horn in on the SCCA franchise by starting a sports car racing series in 1958. The big difference was that this was professional racing for money. The reaction of the SCCA was hypocritical and it threatened sanctions against any racecourse that hosted an event organized by the USAC. The SCCA retaliated by threatening to refuse entry to any USAC license holder in an FIA race. The war went on for some years. The USAC circuit lasted only five years, suffering from sparse fields of very old cars, although crowd attendance was good. The first USAC professional sports car race was at Lime Rock on

September 7, 1958. There were only 16 entries, but with a reported crowd of 17,000, which is hard to believe. Besides the problems of too few cars and drivers, it rained, and Connecticut had a ban on racing in the rain. Lime Rock also had a noise ban, and no racing could be conducted on Sunday before 2 pm.

The most important race event in the US for sports cars became the 12 Hours of Sebring in Florida. General Curtis LeMay of the US Air Force, and head of the Strategic Air Command, was a big race enthusiast and he opened the Air Force bases for racing in an agreement with the SCCA. This solved the SCCA problem of obtaining permission to use public roads, and improved safety standards. Situated on an air force base, the event in Sebring became the best-known race on those flat courses and always saw the European works teams from Ferrari, Maserati, Porsche and Jaguar. But in addition to such circuits there were many events at Watkins Glen, Elkhart Lake, Riverside, Palm Springs, Laguna Seca and Lime Rock. The enthusiasts loved it: the first Riverside race attracted over 50,000 spectators and was the biggest sports car race of that era.

The FIA, which made the rules for all events in Europe and the World Sportscar Championship, was not present in the US and had no authority except for Sebring and the 500 miles of Indianapolis which it sanctioned.

In October 1958, the disagreement between the different parties was resolved, thanks to a very diplomatic Charles Moran who had driven at Le Mans in the 1930s and after the war, and who opened new horizons for US motor sport.

OPPOSITE: Chassis #4506 and the Ferrari 410S (211) beside the famous silver race truck in Riverside in November 1957. All vehicles owned by John Edgar. *(Walter Bäumer Collection)*

This great color photograph from Pomona in March 1959, shows all Maserati cars owned by Texan Ebb Rose and sponsored by Micro-Lube, a manufacturer of fuel and oil additives. Closest to the camera is the battered #4510, in the middle, Lloyd Ruby is leaning over the 300S, chassis #3073 and in the back, the early 300S, chassis #3052 that had been fitted with a Chevy V8 engine. Note the prancing horse painted on both engine hoods. *(Motorsport Images)*

Bill Krause guns #4502 around the circuit at Santa Barbara in September 1959, a track that was well suited for the big 450S. *(Walter Bäumer Collection)*

As in Europe, all US drivers were friends for many years. Lance Reventlow looks to the camera while Chuck Daigh smiles at Jim Rathmann (with hat) and Carroll Shelby in Nassau 1958. *(FORD Museum / Dave Friedman)*

In the 1950's John Edgar Enterprises' silver racing transporter was famous. Team owner John Edgar (with hat) greeted friends and acquaintances on the roof of the truck to watch the races of his cars from there. The truck's interior included four bunks, a kitchenette, a liquor bar, and space for three cars. *(Walter Bäumer Collection)*

...and the music plays, and the girls are dancing. Here at Daytona in April 1959. In front is #4506 with 6.3 liter Pontiac V8 engine, with the Ferrari of Chuck Daigh behind and the Ferrari 121LM of Loyal Katskee in third. *(FORD Museum / Dave Friedman)*

OPPOSITE: Jim Hall's fleet of white race cars at Greenville Avenue in Dallas, Texas: the Lotus 18 Formula junior, chassis #4508 and the Maserati Birdcage #2463. Kneeling are mechanics Frank Lance (left) and Gary Knutson (right) with Foy Barrett standing, who was responsible for the bodies of these cars. Frank Lance reported many years later to one of the authors: "Of all the cars I worked on in the 10 years of my career of racing mechanic, the 450S is still my favorite". *(Bob Jackson)*

One of the main challengers of the Maserati 450S was the Scarab. Here Carroll Shelby battles in #4508 with Lance Reventlow's Scarab driven by Chuck Daigh at Nassau in December 1958. Reventlow was the mastermind behind the Scarab cars. *(FORD Museum / Dave Friedman)*

Carroll Shelby behind the wheel of #4508 in the workshop of the Shelby-Hall dealership in Dallas. Note the seats that were upholstered to match with Carroll Shelby's striped bib overalls. *(Bob Jackson)*

The new #4507 in Sweden ready for the technical inspection by the officials of the 1957 Swedish Grand Prix. Maserati pit-lane boss, Guerino Bertocchi, is in the car. *(Klemantaski Collection)*

THE CARS

4501

OPPOSITE: Moss and his trusted co-driver, journalist Denis Jenkinson, on the ramp in Brescia for the start of the 1956 Mille Miglia. They hoped to repeat their triumph from the previous year when they won the legendary race in a Mercedes 300SLR. *(Walter Bäumer Collection)*

Completed: July 1956
Engine number: #4501
Engine capacity: 4.5 Liter
Color: Red

Finished at the last moment, #3501 headed off to Brescia from behind the factory in Modena. Maserati chief mechanic Guerino Bertocchi is behind the wheel, partnered by an unknown person. Luigi Bellucci follows in the works Maserati 200S. *(Unknown photographer)*

#4501 was initially a 350S, #3501. Stirling Moss with Denis Jenkinson, his companion from his epic Mille Miglia drive with Mercedes-Benz the previous year, was assigned #3501 to compete in the 1956 1,000-mile road race. Two days prior to the Mille Miglia, #3501 was not fully prepared and so Moss, along with Guerino Bertocchi, Maserati's chief mechanic, used a second 350S for a test drive up and down the nearby Raticosa Pass where the car clearly showed its superior speed potential over the 300S. But it had a strong tendency to understeer and, according to Moss, was "very vague" on the front axle, leaving no margin for error, as reported by Jenkinson in his feature in the June 1956 issue of Motor Sport. Moss' car, #3501, was now quickly prepared, including the addition of a spoiler under the nose to stop it from lifting. To the surprise of

the drivers, the spoiler was removed just before the race started, and when Moss complained, he was told that "it just did not look good!"

Nevertheless, Moss and Jenkinson were at the start at Brescia with race number 554 on April 28, 1956. Moss was still not pleased with the way the car handled and treated it with great care, but even on long straights, it was wandering badly from left to right even though the engine was running well. Both men were lucky to escape injury when the car left the road in heavy rain near Antrodoco when the brakes locked while taking a right-hand bend. They crashed through a small stone wall, shot downhill and came to rest by a small tree, 300 feet above a river. #3501 was out of the race.

Terrible weather conditions during the 1956 Mille Miglia and the difficult handling of the car were real problems for Moss. This photo was taken minutes before the crash that ended the race for both drivers. *(Walter Bäumer Collection)*

That was it for #3501 in the 1956 Mille Miglia. Moss and Jenkinson were lucky to survive the crash. *(Walter Breveglieri)*

The Ex-3501, now repaired and labeld as chassis #4501 appeared in Sweden for the Grand Prix 1956. Moss seems unsure what to think of the new T-car. His critical assumption will later be confirmed. The short exhaust pipes had no silencer, and the car had no door on its co-driver-side. *(Bernard Cahier Archives)*

The early version of the V8 engine in #4501 in Sweden. In the back, there is the X-designed frame next to the firewall that was peculiar to this car. *(Walter Bäumer Collection)*

The car was repaired at the factory with a modified body, a stretched chassis to accommodate the big V8 engine of 4,477cc and with 400 bhp. It was renumbered #4501 to reflect the engine number. The "new" car was sent to Sweden with an international customs document or ATA carnet, numbered 4501. #4501 was fitted with a huge bulge on the hood for the carburetors and had four short ''hot rod ''exhausts on both sides which resulted in a terrific engine sound. Everyone was surprised by what rolled out of the factory trucks from Modena. It appeared in Monoposto dressing, with a large T (for "Test") on its front at the 1956 Swedish GP on August 12 at the Råbelövsbanan circuit at Kristianstad near the Baltic Sea, 600 kilometers from Stockholm. Used during practice sessions only, the 450S #4501 showed its weakness. The chassis was not strong enough for the engine's power which caused severe vibrations. With ineffective handling and no reliable brakes, all three Maserati team members, Stirling Moss, Harry Schell and Piero Taruffi, refused to drive it in the race. It was clear that the old 350S chassis was too weak for the big new V8 engine.

That the car in Sweden was based on the 350S chassis is confirmed in the 1958 edition of L'Année Automobile in a feature about the 450S. Another important detail seen on the frame of #3501 and later #4501 are the upright tubes in "X" position in the back of the engine bay, just in front of the firewall. These "X" tubes are clearly based on the 300S/350S chassis design and is not seen on any of the other 450S cars.

Back at the factory after its trip to Sweden, #4501 had its V8 engine removed and a change in its firing order solved the problem of the severe vibrations. The useless chassis and body without engine never raced again and were left outside in the internal courtyards of the factory for years. Meanwhile, the ATA customs carnet, still valid with the registered number 4501, was used to ship a new real 450S to Argentina for the 1,000 km Buenos Aires race in January 1957 (see the #4503 chapter). The same ATA carnet 4501 was used again five months later to ship another 450S, the Zagato coupé (see the #4512 chapter) to France for the 24 Hours of Le Mans. Maserati always tried to get the best out of bureaucracy.

Some eight years later, in 1965, young Californian Tom Meade settled in Modena and came shopping at the factory for the second time (after a first visit and purchase of a 350S in 1960) and bought the abandoned body and #4501 for 80,000 Lire (US$80)!

In an interview given to the journalist, Chad Glass, in July 2012, the late Tom Meade remembered: "At the Maserati factory there was a second 350S out back and I bought it for US$80. It was a prototype for the 450S V8 which is worth between 7 and 8 million dollars today. I realized that these cars were just left around the place like that, as the junkman wouldn't take them. There were too many different kinds of metal in them. And it was too expensive a process to dismantle them. So I bought the cars for the value of the junk metal."

The full package without its Swedish rear and front bonnet was certified by the factory as chassis 350S-10 as seen on the "Certificato d'Origine" signed by Adolfo Orsi Sr. and issued on October 19, 1965: "Telaio Maserati Tipo 350/SI N°10 con carrozzeria e parti meccaniche, escluso motore."

In the meantime, Meade had already sold his car on August 15, 1965, to his friend Nile F. Moss and received the full payment on October 29, 1965. With the help of Modenese shops, Meade had installed a V8 Corvette engine and a 5-speed Ferrari transaxle from a 1955 Mondial. The hybrid car was set up at Gentilini's restoration workshop in Modena for road use as invoiced to Nile Moss on September 6, 1965, and reappeared with a large glass windshield, a new passenger door and two new bonnets front and rear.

The Maserati was shipped to the USA and was sold by Nile Moss on May 26,1970 to Gerald H. Satterfield from Nevada City, California who used it as his daily driver. Then the well-known collector and Maserati afficionado, Franco Lombardi from Genoa, Italy bought the car on July 29, 1981 from Satterfield while he was traveling in the USA. Lombardi shipped the car to his homeland and started a long process of restoration. A pair of small photographs show the car when it landed back in Italy, most probably in the factory since a V8 engine is standing nearby on a shelf.

The car was inspected by Officine Alfieri Maserati S.p.A in February 1983 and now keenly aware of its own provenance, they helped with a full restoration. Ex-factory engineers helped source a period Maserati V8, from a racing hydroplane owned by Count Agusta. It was engine number 4519, a Tipo 59 with a 110-mm bore for a total of 6.4 liters. "It develops a rather exuberant amount of power but is easier to handle because of its 'softer' marine unit cam profiles," said Franco Lombardi. In April 2014 the #4501 was auctioned by RM at Monte Carlo but remained unsold. Shortly afterwards, Franco Lombardi, after 33 years of ownership, sold his car to a collector in the USA.

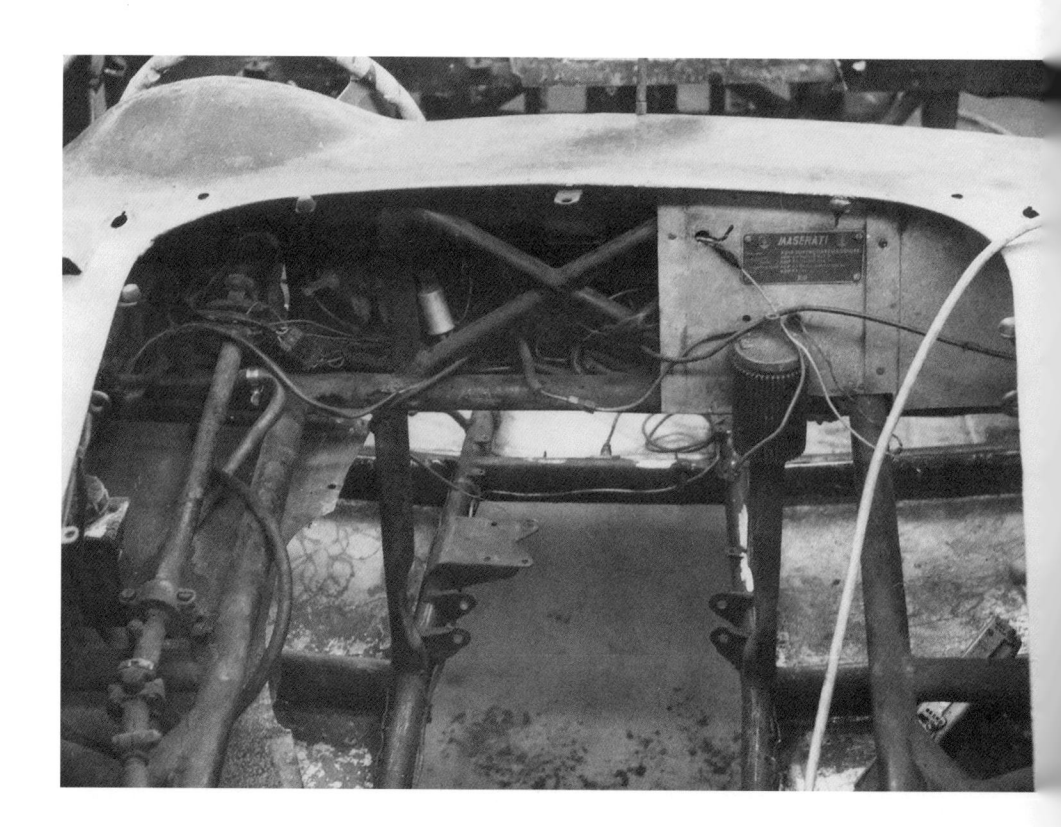

OPPOSITE: This photograph shows the rear chassis section in the engine bay of #4501 in "X" design when the car was owned by Franco Lombardi. *(Unknown photographers)*

The car without its body in the Orsi workshop just after the chassis restoration was completed but with the engine fitted. *(Franco Lombardi Collection)*

4501 RACE HISTORY

| 29 | April 1956 | Mille Miglia | Stirling Moss/Denis Jenkinson (no. 554) DNF, crash |
| 12 | Aug. 1956 | Swedish GP, Kristianstad | Practice with Stirling Moss, Harry Schell, Piero Taruffi (no. T) DNS |

4502

Completed: October 29, 1956
Engine: #4502
Engine capacity: 4.2 Liter
Color: Red with a black and white center stripe

Tony Parravano, an Italian born near Rome in 1917 who later immigrated to the US, was the first owner of #4502, the first 450S that was made by Maserati. Parravano, who made his fortune in the construction business in California after the Second World War, was an important customer of both Maserati and Ferrari. He bought a Ferrari 375 MM, a 750 Monza and a 121 but after some disagreements with Enzo Ferrari, he turned his attention to the Trident cars in 1953, buying an A6GCS. Money was not an issue for him, and Maserati gave him a warm welcome.

During 1955 and 1956, this hot-tempered "Americano" purchased a 150S, a 250F, a 300S and one of the three 350S, a pair of 4.2-Tipo 54 Indy engines. This influx of cash from Parravano helped Maserati considerably in the development of its cars and allowed the company to experiment with new designs, including the new 450S with its powerful V8 engine. Parravano then had the most competitive race stable in America called the Scuderia Parravano whose trademark was a black stripe along the length of the cars, framed on each side by a small white one. Among his drivers were Masten Gregory, Jack McAfee, Jimmy Bryan and Texan, Carroll Shelby. In its September 1956 issue, the US magazine *Speed Age* estimated the value of his racing cars to be US$300,000, an incredible amount in those days. His stock of parts was valued at US$12,000, and Parravano was quoted as saying: "… I have more parts than the New York (Maserati) distributor and nearly as many parts as the factory…!" He was clearly the major force in Californian racing.

Parravano visited Italy a couple of times, and in 1956 he discussed the new V8 project Maserati had in mind in their headquarters in Modena. He finally

OPPOSITE: Maserati test driver Umberto Stradi drives #4502 at the Aerautodromo in Modena, a small race circuit within an airfield in the center of the city. The car bears its early coachwork with the very short exhaust pipes before Fantuzzi had worked out in its final design. *(Unknown photographer)*

A cold and windy day at Willow Springs in January 1957. Owner Tony Parravano, facing the camera, is in discussion with his mechanics who are working on his Maserati 350S (#3502). In the foreground is his 450S, #4502. Parravano would never see either car race. *(Jack McAfee)*

OPPOSITE: The engine bay of #4502 with its early upright carburetor specification. Note the seats covered with unique light-colored cloth with dark piping. *(Getty Images)*

Owner Jack Brumby tried his #4502 in practice at Pomona on January 31, 1959, and quickly found that the car was too powerful for him to drive. *(Walter Bäumer Collection)*

The ex-Parravano 450S, driven by Dan Gurney, in the middle of the field during the press parade in Riverside, June 1957. Leading the pack is a Jaguar XKSS and Ken Miles in his Porsche 550 (no. 50). *(Will Edgar Motorsport Archive)*

Pomona, March 7, 1959. Bill Krause in #4502 with new owner Jack Brumby. Behind the car is Lloyd Ruby in his Chevy-powered Maserati 300S. In the back right is #4508 with Carroll Shelby. Krause was the winner of the race. *(Walter Bäumer Collection)*

Again Pomona, 1959 when Carroll Shelby leads in #4508, followed by Chuck Daigh in a Kurtis/Buick. In third is Bill Krause driving #4502, with George Amik in the yellow Mercedes-Benz owned by Chuck Porter behind. Only Daigh and Krause saw the finish line. *(Allen R. Kuhn)*

Bill Krause guns #4502 through a corner during practice at the Kiwanis GP at Riverside in July 1959. Following the damage in Pomona, the car had been repaired but was now painted in black primer. *(Walter Bäumer Collection)*

OPPOSITE: A 450S in gold was a rare sight. After the car had been repainted overnight, Krause seemed to have hit something during the race. The German flag is upside down, by the way. *(Allen R. Kuhn)*

ordered his car, #4502, directly at the factory. Fitted with unpainted and roughly made coachwork, the car was driven by Maserati test driver Umberto Stradi at the Aerautodromo, the small racetrack that was in the infield of the airport in Modena. Fantuzzi reworked the coachwork and the car emerged with elegant lines. Its design clearly shows the influence of the late 300S.

#4502 was officially completed on October 29, 1956, and tested again at the Aerautodromo. One small detail that separated #4502 from all the other 450S are the two small oval holes on its back instead of either three or four openings. It was the only 450S that was made with a single front screen, a tonneau over the co-driver's seat, a two-piece rear hood and an oil filler cap on top of its right fender.

Maserati had painted the car in its Corsa-red color but with the Parravano trademark black and white stripes. Furthermore, the car had a unique front grille with three horizontal bars that held the Trident logo in the middle, never seen before or since on any Maserati. On November 23, #4502 was on its way to its impatient new owner in Inglewood, California, together with two 4.2-liter spare engines. Parravano got a huge discount from Maserati and finally paid $7,000 for the entire package.

January 6, 1957 was a gray, cool day and Parravano had organized test sessions at Willow Springs in the Californian desert. He transported almost all his race cars there to be driven by Bob Drake, Jack McAfee, Richie Ginther, Dan Gurney and others. A photograph with Jack McAfee in the car was published in MotoRacing on February 8, 1957, and was referred to as the "bomb."

The car was entered in the parade lap for the press opening of the Riverside racetrack on June 19, 1957, with Dan Gurney behind the wheel. But in the meantime, Tony Parravano was struck in huge legal problems with the IRS, the US tax administration. Everything around him was always "big time" but paying taxes was not on his agenda. In April 1957, he fled to Mexico, and in a daring move, several of his cars were transported there by night where they spent years in storage. The other cars, including #4502, were confiscated by the IRS and sold in two separate auctions in September 1958.

Tony Parravano, the big gambler and race fanatic, had to face a court case set by the IRS, but he never appeared in the courtroom. He was last seen on April 8, 1960, and then disappeared forever, most likely a victim of some of his business partners. Jack Brumby became the new owner of #4502. He owned Italia Motors at 1070 Myra Avenue, East Hollywood, California, a company that was financed by Dr. Rey Martinez. They each paid $3,000 for the car.

The Maserati, still in Parravano's livery, was entered in its first race at Pomona, a short circuit in California, on January 31 to February 1,1959. Brumby brought the car out on the track during the practice session, but after some laps, he immediately found that his skills were not good enough to drive the 450S.

Brumby and Martinez hired Bill Krause, a talented and fast race driver who previously had driven Jaguar D-Types and other potent cars. Many years later, Krause reported: "...I practiced by running it up and down the parking lot a

couple of times. [...] it was huge! It was a truck. It steered so hard that I had to work out all the time with those springs that you stress. At Pomona, it broke the steering brackets right off the frame. There was something wrong with the steering of that prototype. You had to steer it by throttle, as you just could not turn the wheel. The brakes did not bother me, and it had lots of horsepower and torque, ideal for a track like Riverside."

With no real practice driving the car, he came in fifth overall in race 9 against strong opposition. Krause, as good as he was, quickly learned how to handle the truck and in the main race he finished second behind Richie Ginther in a Ferrari 335S.

Brumby and Martinez advertised #4502 for sale in the February 1959 issue of *Autosport*, including many spare parts and an engine, that was perhaps a spare unit that Parravano had ordered for the car. It remained unsold and was repainted bright silver with a dark blue stripe and red borders, promoting "Italia Motors SpL" on its right front fender.

The next venue for Krause and his truck was again Pomona on March 7-8, 1959 for the Examiner GP attended by 40,000 visitors. The starting grid saw eight Maseratis, among them no less than four 450Ss: Hal Ullrich in #4504, Carroll Shelby in #4508 and Ebb Rose in his #4509. Krause was the fastest of the four and was leading the main race followed by Ken Miles in a Porsche 550RS. But bad luck happened to the silver-blue #4502. Krause reported later: "The center bolt in the rear spring broke. A leaf spring came out and cut the right rear tire. It blew and the car did a 360. I just missed a large telephone pole. It scared me as I thought the car was going into the crowd and the only protection was snow fencing. In the end, the car just slid by the fence, pointing the right way again. It all happened so fast that I did not realize what had happened. I just stuck it in gear and got back on the throttle. While I was on the back straight, rubber started flying off: bang, bang! By then, I realized I had lost my rear tire. With only minimal pit communication, I didn't know how many laps were left, so I came in to have the wheel changed. The crew told me just to go on, as there was only one lap to go [...] I bent every corner of that Maserati during the race. The track was not really suited for that type of car. Once you were committed to a corner, you could not start changing your mind in the 4.5."

Four months later, on July 19, 1959, #4502 was entered in the Kiwanis GP at the Riverside race circuit in California. Bill Krause practiced the car painted in black primer due to the damage at Pomona, and it was freshly painted overnight in gold with a dark blue stripe with red borders and had lost its significant front grille. Riverside had a terrible heatwave that day.

OPPOSITE: Bill Krause was the master of #4502. He was at Santa Barbara in September 1959. *(Walter Bäumer Collection)*

A rare photograph. On October 16,1960 for the Times GP, Dick Morgensen in his Ferrari 250TR chases Chuck Kessinger in #4502, that now appears in a flashy copper color. The 450S and the Ferrari were fourth and fifth fastest in the Consolation race but that was not fast enough to qualify for the race. *(Jean-François Blachette Collection)*

OPPOSITE: Back at Riverside for the Consolation race on October 15, 1961. #4502 was now painted silver with a big red stripe and driven by Chuck Kessinger who finished in seventh place. *(Paul Freier)*

The aging #4502 in front of Lee Toxel's shop at Myrna Avenue in Los Angeles. The car still bears the old race number used by Kessinger at Riverside in October 1961. For his last two races, the "3" was pasted over with a "5." *(Walter Bäumer Collection)*

#4502 was owned by Cameron Millar in the late 1980s. He commissioned dark-blue paint for the car. Note the chromed cover that is mounted on the side over the exhaust pipes. *(Walter Bäumer Collection)*

On lap 28 and in second place, Krause had to be removed from his car: "It was actually fume poisoning. The crew had put an extra air scoop on the body, because of the hot race conditions, but the result was that all the oil and gas fumes from the engine compartment went straight into the cockpit. It put me to sleep. I was dozing off going down the straight."

Pete Woods took over the car but had the same problem and could not stand the conditions and so #4502 was out of the race. On September 5-6, 1959, Krause was on the grid for the races at Santa Barbara. He clearly won the sprint race, but during the main race on Sunday, he had bad luck: the car became very difficult to handle and Krause came to the pits after 15 laps. His mechanics checked the car and found that one of the shock absorbers was loose, hanging from the frame. It was the end of the race for #4502 and the last time that Bill Krause was behind its steering wheel. #4502 was aging now, and a new generation of cars were stronger and more competitive.

In 1960, the car again changed its color and was painted a flashy copper red. Chuck Kessinger, a Californian who drove a Fiat-Abarth in Sebring in 1958, drove it at Riverside on October 16, 1960, finishing fourth overall in the Consolation race but was not good enough to qualify for the race.

Kessinger was back in #4502 in the 200-mile race at Pomona on March 11-12, 1961. It was now painted bright silver with a red stripe that became wide over the entire nose section, and the old 450S finished on seventh position in the main race, after having spin on lap 2 while on fourth. On October 15, 1961, Chuck Kessinger was back at the wheel of #4502 for the Times GP, but could not qualify for the GP race, having only finished as ninth in the consolation race.

On March 2-3, 1962, Kessinger participated again in the SCCA Pacific Coast Club race at Riverside. In race 3, he was the last car to finish but in race 14, he did better and just missed the podium, finishing in fourth place. From then on, no other race for #4502 is recorded. It had a very brief appearance in the 1964 Elvis Presley movie "Viva Las Vegas."

The car was probably stored for some years by owner Rey Martinez until he sold it to a Lee Toxel, perhaps a dealer who was also from Los Angeles. He offered the car for sale with an asking price of US$3,000 and finally sold it to Bill Grimiscin from York, Pennsylvania, who restored the car in 1967. He installed a strange exhaust system and sold it to Tiny Gould in Philadelphia. Early in 1968, it was purchased by enthusiast and collector Joel Finn from New York. He was contacted by Cameron Millar, a Maserati enthusiast, amateur racer, and important member of the Maserati Club UK from Northaw in Great Britain, and the car crossed the Atlantic to Cameron Millar's garage. He used #4502 in some events and offered it for sale in August 1975 by dealer Rod Leach's Nostalgia, Hertford Heath, UK who advertised it in the magazine *Thoroughbred & Classic Cars* in the same month.

Count Hubertus von Dönhoff from Munich, Germany, an amateur racer and founder of the Oldtimer Grand Prix at the Nürburgring, bought it and gave it to respected mechanic and driver Tony Merrick for restoration. It was painted dark

blue. No other 450S changed its color so often as #4502! The nobleman participated in the 1991 Mille Miglia.

In 1996, collector and amateur race driver Hartmut Ibing from Düsseldorf purchased the still dark blue 450S, drove it in some events, and kept it for eleven years. During his ownership, a major engine overhaul was done by specialist Capricorn in Mönchengladbach, Germany. They redesigned the crankshaft and finally, it was probably the most competitive 450S in those days. Bernd Hahne from Düsseldorf, a talented amateur racer of everything that was fast handled the big car perfectly, drove it in four races, and won them all.

In 2007, the car was sold to amateur racer and businessman, Willy Balz, from Southern Germany. He was a good driver but did not use it very often. Balz was facing financial troubles in 2013 and the car was sold to a collector from Switzerland. A cosmetic restoration followed and the car, still in its non-original dark blue paint, was entered in the 2014 Concours d'Elegance at Villa d'Este where it won the "Best of Show" award. It should be noted that #4502 still has its original coachwork fitted.

OPPOSITE: Chassis #4502 on the old circuit of the Nürburgring in 2004. *(Walter Bäumer)*

4502 RACE HISTORY

06	Jan.	1957	Willow Springs test day	Bob Drake/Jack McAfee/Richie Ginther/Dan Gurney
19	June	1957	Press parade, Riverside, California	Dan Gurney
31	Jan.	1959	Pomona, California, race 9	Bill Krause (no. 53) 5.OA
01	Feb.	1959	Pomona, California, sprint	Bill Krause (no. 53) 2.OA
07	March	1959	Pomona, California, race 6	Bill Krause (no. 53) 1.OA
08	March	1959	Los Angeles Examiner GP, Pomona, California	Bill Krause (no. 53) 1.OA
19	July	1959	Kiwanis GP, Riverside, California	Bill Krause/Pete Woods (no. 53) DNF
05	Sept.	1959	Santa Barbara, California, race 9	Bill Krause (no. 127) 1.OA
06	Sept.	1959	Santa Barbara, California, race 17	Bill Krause (no. 127) DNF
16	Oct.	1960	Consolation race, Times GP, Riverside, California	Chuck Kessinger (no. 41) 4.OA, DNQ
12	March	1961	Club race, Pomona, California	Chuck Kessinger (no. 10) 7.OA
15	Oct.	1961	Consolation race, Riverside, California	Chuck Kessinger (no. 33) 9.OA
03	March	1962	Cal Club race, Riverside, California, race 3	Chuck Kessinger (no. 53) 6.OA
04	March	1962	Cal Club race, Riverside, California, race 14	Chuck Kessinger (no. 53) 4.OA

4503

Completed: December 18, 1956
Engine: #4503
Engine capacity: 4.5 Liter
Color: Red

#4503 was the second chassis built in the series and the first works car and it was one of the most beautiful race cars that ever rolled out of the gates of the Maserati factory in Modena. Like all factory cars, it came without a headrest. #4503 began its tumultuous sporting career in the 1,000 km Buenos Aires, held on January 20, 1957.

Juan Manuel Fangio had just left Ferrari and had signed with Maserati to drive its cars in the Formula 1 World Championship. Just days before the 1,000 km race, he had won the Argentinian Grand Prix in his Maserati 250F and could not resist driving the new weapon from Modena. He raced the 450S with race number 2 and it confirmed the superiority seen during practice sessions against the 3.5-liter Ferrari 290MM. The Ferrari team protested the speed of the Maserati 450S, and so overnight the organizers built a chicane or additional curve to slow the cars down. Fangio still cranked out an incredible lap of 106 mph. It was here that he gave the 450S its nickname, "Bazooka."

In the race, co-driver Stirling Moss was easily in the lead using the power of the Maserati, and the Ferraris were outclassed, losing 9 seconds per lap. When Moss handed over to Fangio, it was obvious that the Maserati would probably win. Unfortunately, several laps after mid-race, the Maserati came into the pits and retired with a broken gearbox. It was a more than lucky win for Ferrari.

All evidence suggests that this 450S was #4503, completed at the factory on December 18, 1956, and having traveled to Argentina under the valid ATA carnet #4501 which was still valid for the ugly 450S prototype, that had been used for the 1956 Swedish GP (see the #4501 chapter).

Examination of the period photographs of the cockpit and lateral reinforcements of the frame allows one to advance this hypothesis. Also, details on the bodywork, such as three oval cuts in the tail, or three rows of the unique four horizontal cuts in the front bonnet help to identify the Buenos Aires car and the car that was used later in Sebring as the same 450S. Moreover, an additional third filler tap just behind the driver's seat was already added at Buenos Aires, a trademark of #4503 all during its racing career: a feature not seen on any other 450S.

Stirling Moss wrote in his *Scrapbook 1956-1960* about the race: "The following Sunday it was the sports-car race, the Buenos Aires 1,000 Kilometer, in which I was to share with Fangio the wheel of the new 4.5-titre V8 Maserati, the 450S. The organizers had decided to run the race on the Costanera circuit, which had been used in 1951 before the Autodrome was built. It was 6.3 miles to the lap, and the straight doubled back on itself, so in effect there was a two-way traffic system with cars going both ways at around 160 mph. As if this were not dangerous enough in itself, the circuit was also unmarked and very bumpy. [...] As to the race itself, although I did not win, I reckon it was one of the best races I ever had.

"When the flag fell, the 450S simply streaked away from the Ferraris, and by lap 10, I was a good 60 seconds ahead of Masten Gregory. By thirty laps, I was two and a quarter minutes up. The car called for a considerable amount of discretion in its handling on this circuit, which was a difficult one, with high-speed corners as well as slow ones, because of its tremendous acceleration and maximum speed; I do not think there is any doubt that I could have gone much quicker if it had been necessary to do so. I was called in [...] and Fangio took over the car, and by the forty-eighth lap, he had lapped the entire field except for Eugenio Castellotti, who had taken over from Gregory about the same time as I handed over to Fangio.

"However, it was not long before the car began to give trouble, and eventually, on the fifty-seventh lap, the gearbox gave up the ghost. The clutch-operating mechanism had broken, and Fangio had been changing gears without it, which was too much for the gearbox.

"Castellotti went into the lead, with the Behra/Menditéguy 3-liter Maserati lying fourth. It was not until the sixty-fifth lap that I took over the 3-liter and started to chase the Ferraris, who counter-attacked by calling in Castellotti on the sixty-seventh lap and giving his car to Musso whilst Castellotti took over the de Portago/Collins car. Oddly enough, the 3-liter was a car far more suited to the circuit and much easier to handle, although not nearly as quick. Anyway, I found it much easier to drive the 3-liter on the limit than to nurse the 4.5 [...]."

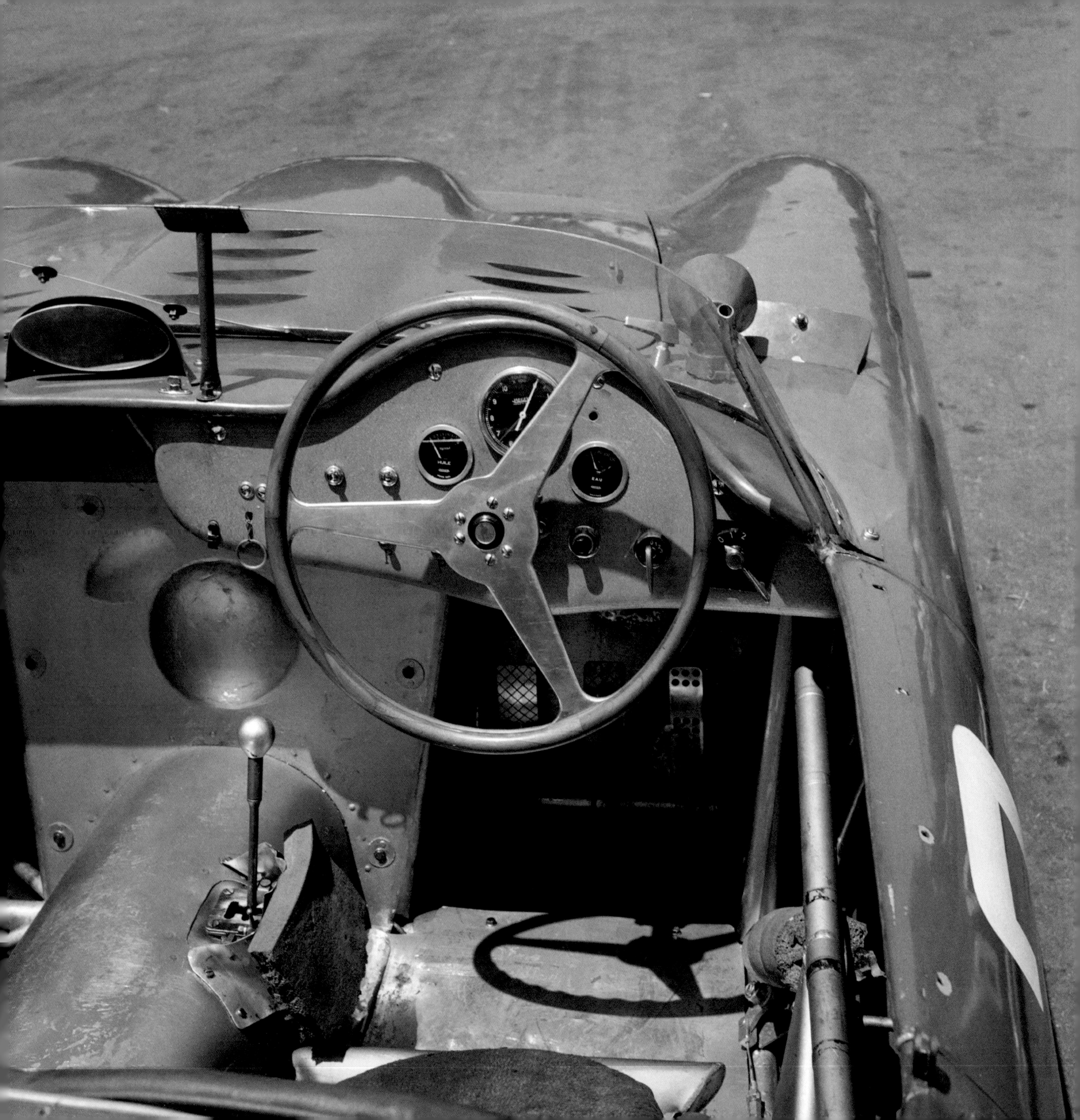

OPPOSITE: Maserati mechanics changing spark plugs on the engine of #4503 in the paddock of the 1,000 km of Buenos Aires early in 1957. *(Walter Bäumer Collection)*

"Should I take the big one or the old 300S?" Stirling Moss looked skeptical in the pits before the 1,000 km of Buenos Aires in January 1957. *(Walter Bäumer Collection)*

OPPOSITE: Fangio tested #4503 in Buenos Aires in 1957. The great lines of the car were another Fantuzzi masterpiece. *(Klemantaski Collection)*

The start of the 1957 1,000 km race in Buenos Aires. Moss blew off the entire Ferrari and Jaguar opposition, but at the end of the race, Masten Gregory in his Ferrari 290MM (no. 10) was the winner. *(Klemantaski Collection)*

Moss in #4503 on the apex of a corner, near thousands of spectators who lined the circuit with only minimal security barriers. *(Klemantaski Collection)*

A marvelous shot of #4503 in the workshop in Florida where the Maserati mechanics prepared their cars for the 1957 12 Hours of Sebring race. To achieve better aerodynamics for an even higher top speed, the air holes for cooling the brakes have been covered. Note the additional yellow third headlight, which is mounted on the lower lip of in the radiator opening. *(Revs Institute)*

OPPOSITE: A fantastic shot that shows #4503 in the Sebring pitlane in 1957. All significant details are visible: the unique filler cap directly behind the driver's seat, the twelve air intakes on the engine bonnet and the small leather straps to hold the rear bonnet. Note the foam that is taped around one side tube of the car to protect the driver's leg. Car no. 20 is the 300S, #3071 of Moss. *(Karl Ludvigsen)*

Fangio steps out of the car for Jean Behra at the 1957 Sebring race. The 12 air out-takes on the car's front bonnet were a detail that no other 450S had. *(Bernard Cahier Archives)*

Guerino Bertocchi checks the rear wheels during a refueling pit stop for #4503. The three oval openings in the rear of the car are a significant detail in its later history to distinguish it from other cars. Legendary French photographer, Bernard Cahier, with cap, stands directly in front of the car. *(Revs Institute)*

After its retirement in Argentina, #4503 was back in Italy for changes to the body: a larger radiator opening with a lower lip, a fourth cut on both sides of the rear fenders, two leather straps on the rear to hold the bonnet and a small, strange air intake drilling the windshield.

The next big event was the 12 Hours of Sebring in Florida on March 23, 1957, which attracted all teams because of the large prize and starting money. The Italian rivals made great efforts to prepare their cars well for this most important sports car race since winning here would clearly affect sales on the American market. The June issue of *MCA RACING NEWS*, the official publication of the Maserati Corporation of America wrote about the factory team: "...The Sebring expedition involved four cars, more than five tons of spares and miscellaneous material, eight drivers, eight mechanics, and approximately ten other people..." The package consisted of two 300S, a 450S and a 250S. All cars were driven by mechanics on the open roads to the race from the local workshop where they had been maintained.

In that event, Maserati probably had its strongest team of the 1950s: Fangio with Behra again in the big V8, Moss with Schell in the first 300S, Carroll Shelby with Roy Salvadori in the second 3-liter, and Bonnier with Giorgio Scarlatti in the 2.5-liter car. Moss had tested #4503, and he knew about the 450S's brake problem and therefore preferred to drive in the 300S. Everybody was again stunned by the power of the "Bazooka," but they expected the car to be unreliable.

All Ferrari works team drivers were interviewed before practice for the vinyl album *"Sounds of Sebring 1957"* about what they are thinking about the "big 4.5" of Maserati. All of them clearly doubted that the car would be reliable. Wolfgang von Trips was skeptical but said that it "...is very, very fast and if the car does not break down, it has the greatest chance of winning the race."

By invitation, both Fangio and Moss tried out in practice the advanced Corvette SS designed by Zora Arkus-Duntov. Both drivers were impressed by its power, but Moss clearly stated in an interview that he liked "his" 300S more.

The headlights of #4503 were covered with cardboard attached with long strips of tape and an additional headlamp had been mounted in the radiator opening. Behra went out for the first stint in the race. He started cautiously, following Guerino Bertocchi's instructions, "Do not exceed 6,100 rpm. At this speed, you have 375 bhp...." The French driver was in second place behind Peter Collins's Ferrari after the first hour of racing. Behra accelerated, and after two laps, he overtook the Ferrari. Eleven hours later, the 450S, now driven by Fangio crossed the line first, two laps ahead of Stirling Moss-Harry Schell's 300S. For the 450S, the only warning was a 65-second penalty due to the number of mechanics working on the car during a pit stop. Thanks to this result, Maserati was now leading the Sports Car Championship with 14 points, with Ferrari having 11. The Sebring win was the most important result for any of the ten 450S chassis built.

Back again in Italy, #4503 received a new axle and was prepared for Jean Behra to be entered at the famous Mille Miglia with race number 536. Behra went out for a practice run with factory driver Giorgio Scarlatti in the co-driver's

seat who was frightened to death by Behra's driving style combined with the endless power of the car. Scarlatti then used a 300S for the race. Then Moss and Jenkinson practiced as well in #4503 a few days before the start in Brescia, but later received their new #4505 only ready at the last minute before the legendary road race.

Unfortunately, on the eve of the start, Maserati lost one of its best assets when Jean Behra took #4503 for a final test run. The Frenchman was cruising at 250 km/h on an open road when the Maserati collided with a truck. Thrown out of the car, Behra suffered some bruises and a broken wrist. Answering journalist Hans Tanner who asked what he had done after crashing the Maserati, Behra said: "I looked through the wreck, picked up my money, my cigarette lighter and my plastic ear (he had lost his right ear in 1955 when he crashed in Ireland in his 300S) and thumbed a lift to the nearest hospital."

A careful examination of the period images confirms that the damaged 450S was #4503. Despite its poor condition, the car was repaired in time for racing at the Nürburgring 1,000 km two weeks later and the 24 Hours of Le Mans. The identity of the 450S seems to have been confirmed by the testimony of mechanic Anacleto "Cleto" Grandi in June 2019 to one of the authors. Grandi had just joined Maserati in April 1957, and his first job as a chassis specialist was to repair a 450S that had crashed: "We remade an identical chassis by giving it the same chassis number." There was no other damaged 450S than #4503.

Then, on May 26, 1957, despite his dislike for endurance racing, Fangio was back in Germany for the 1,000 km on the Nürburgring to replace Jean Behra who was still in hospital. During practice, the Argentinian star driver achieved the fastest lap with #4503 which was entered for Harry Schell and Hans Herrmann with race number 2. Schell made a good start and was past the pits on the opening lap in second place behind the Aston Martin of Tony Brooks. After the retirement of his 450S (see the #4505 chapter) with race number 1, Fangio moved on to #4503, replacing Herrmann. On lap 17, Fangio was in second place but soon brought the car back to the pits with a loose oil tank. Repairing it made him lose two laps, and when Moss took over, the 450S had dropped to seventeenth place. One lap later, the car came in again and retired with a split oil tank.

The next race was the prestigious 24 Hours of Le Mans. The car appeared with a smaller radiator opening that had both side areas covered with red aluminum parts. #4503 was driven in practice by Fangio, and with a new record speed of 203.326 km/h, it shattered the previous record of 199.176 km/h achieved by Mike Hawthorn in his Ferrari 335S V12 works car. It was the first time the 200km/h barrier was broken. The Maserati team was in a good mood.

At 4:00 pm on June 22, 1957, the now recovered Jean Behra with race number 2 was off to a bad start and was seventeenth after two laps. Thanks to the brutish 410 bhp of the 4.5-liter powerplant, he performed a spectacular comeback to second place after one hour of driving behind the Ferrari of Mike Hawthorn and Luigi Musso. Behra was quickly reducing the gap when the Hawthorn pitted for a tire change. The Frenchman was now leading, ahead of Moss' 450S Berlinetta

Maserati chief mechanic, Guerino Bertocchi, hugs Juan Manuel Fangio, the winner, together with Jean Behra, in the 1957 12 Hours of Sebring. It was one of the most important wins for Maserati in the 1950s. *(Walter Bäumer Collection)*

TOP AND OPPOSITE: The well dressed Valerio Colotti, the famous gearbox engineer at Maserati, inspect the well used #4503 after it came back from Sebring and was in need of a refreshment. The lower square lip of the radiator opening appears to have been damaged during transportation and was subsequently straightened before the car was practiced and crashed before the start of the Mille Miglia. *(Walter Bäumer Collection)*

Maserati works driver, Jean Behra, tested #4503 just prior to the 1957 Mille Miglia on public roads when he collided with a truck. He was thrown out of the car, survived but could not start in the legendary race. *(Walter Bäumer Collection)*

Beside Moss in #4505 Harry Schell in #4503 with race number 2 took the start at the Nürburgring for the 1,000 km race in 1957. Later the car was retired due to damage of the oil tank. *(Unknown photographer)*

Fangio passes the Ferrari 500TRC of Gotfried Köchert and Edwin Bauer that had just exited the pitlane at the 1,000 km race on the Nürburgring. Chassis #4503 was used by all team drivers but did not see the finish, while the Ferrari came home thirteenth overall. *(Walter Bäumer Collection)*

Fangio actually only had a contract with Maserati for their Grand Prix races, but he also drove in some of their sports car races. He was not nominated by Maserati for Le Mans, but was there and tested #4503, his winning car at Sebring, before the start of the legendary 24-hour race. *(Klemantaski Collection)*

OPPOSITE: Two Maserati mechanics and Guerino Bertocchi make some adjustments to #4503's engine after practice at Le Mans while Jean Behra (with goggles) watches. Note the additional headlamp that is mounted to the lower lip of the radiator opening. The opening itself is now smaller to improve the aerodynamics of the car. *(Walter Bäumer Collection)*

Fearless Jean Behra corners #4503 in Le Mans. His driving style was always spectacular and he liked driving the big Maserati. Note the c entral headlamp repainted blue for the French team Behra-Simon. *(Bernard Cahier Archives)*

OPPOSITE: A rare photograph of André Simon, who drove
#4503 in Le Mans for a brief time. *(Michel Bollée Collection)*

André Simon talks to an official after he has parked #4503 next to the
track while a Maserati mechanic checks the car. *(Motorsportimages.com)*

Trusted part-time factory driver Giorgio Scarlatti gunned #4503 around a corner of the Aerautodromo in Modena, testing the car before the "Race of Two Worlds" in Monza. *(Hans Tanner)*

OPPOSITE: Monza was a high-speed track. For the Race of Two Worlds, Maserati further improved the aerodynamics on #4503 by covering the holes for brake cooling and a single windshield. The car still had the smaller radiator opening from the previous event at Le Mans. Jean Behra in his trademark red pullover, talks to Bertocchi after the car has been unloaded from the factory truck. *(Klemantaski Collection)*

Four factory mechanics are working on the rear of the jacked-up #4503 during practice for the 1957 Swedish Grand Prix. *(Klemantaski Collection)*

OPPOSITE: A great photograph of Stirling Moss on the apex of a long corner in Kristianstad during the 1957 Swedish Grand Prix. *(Klemantaski Collection)*

OPPOSITE: #4503 crossed the Atlantic Ocean as part of the Maserati Equipe for the last round of the Sportscar World Championship at the Venezuela Grand Prix in Caracas in November 1957. Now it had its open holes for brake cooling again and its wide front screen, but it also had a round lower lip. The car looked fresh and clean during practice but did not see the end of the race in that condition. *(Walter Bäumer Collection)*

Factory driver Giorgio Scarlatti shouts something to Jean Behra, who is waiting in #4503 for his practice session to start in Caracas. *(Jean-Marc Teissedre Collection)*

British racer Tony Brooks took the car on some practice laps for the Grand Prix in Caracas. It would be his only ride in a 450S. *(Walter Bäumer Collection)*

coupé (see the #4512 chapter). Behra entered the pits for refueling and gave his seat to his compatriot André Simon who came out still in the lead but immediately noticed that the brakes and the clutch were malfunctioning. The hard driving by Behra had obviously left its marks. Simon did not finish his first lap. At the end of Les Hunaudières, a universal joint broke, piercing the fuel tank. Showered with fuel, Simon managed to stop the car, avoiding a fire.

In less than three hours, the Maserati's chances had been destroyed. Soon it would be the same for Ferrari, leaving a Jaguar D-Type to win.

Interviewed in 1990, André Simon remembered his participation with Maserati in the 1957 Le Mans event: "It was a great thing; it was going strong! There was a gear reducer, an overdrive with ten speeds. With Behra, we had some bad luck. You had to see the type of organization at Maserati. This car had won the 12 Hours of Sebring. After that race, the factory had simply changed the spark plugs and retightened the clutch stroke, that was all!" This comment says it all.

The next event was the "Race of the Two Worlds" organized on June 30, 1957, on the fast Monza circuit where the best roadsters coming from the USA would battle against the best European cars. Maserati entered two cars for Behra: a 250F Formula 1 car, fitted with a 3.5-liter V12 engine and #4503 fitted with a 4.2-liter engine, equipped with Hallibrand magnesium wheels and Firestone tires, dressed as a Monoposto with a small windshield and a metal tonneau cover. After an unsuccessful test with the 250F for qualifying, Behra took the 450S for a few laps, but the transmission blew, putting an end to the Maserati attempt to qualify! Once again Maserati came insufficiently prepared for the 500-mile race.

Back in the standard Biposto dressing, #4503 was then shipped to Kristianstad on the edge of the Baltic Sea, to take part in the Swedish GP on the Råbelövsbanan circuit for a 6-Hour race. At this stage in the Championship, Maserati could not afford to lose, and the stakes of the sixth race in the series were high. Because of the best four results rule, Maserati still had a chance to be crowned at the last race in November in Caracas if it could win the GP of Sweden. If Ferrari was the winner, going to Venezuela would be useless. Two 450S were entered in Sweden: #4503 for Moss and Harry Schell with race number 8 and the new #4507 with race number 7 for Behra and Moss again. After the transmission problems encountered at the Nürburgring and Le Mans, Maserati took care of the 450S universal joints and half shafts. After an excellent start with Moss leading the race, #4503 retired once again with a broken transmission after three hours while Schell was at the wheel. Fortunately for the Maserati team, the sister car #4507 won the race with the striking pair Behra-Moss and therefore they were back in the hunt for the World title.

Moss, after he had crashed his 450S, took over #4503 from Jean Behra. The car had caught fire after refueling, but it was still a "hot" seat for Moss, as the fire had not been completely extinguished and was still smoldering. In this photograph, traces of the fire can still be seen on the rear of the car. *(Walter Bäumer Collection)*

Back in Modena, #4503 was refurbished with a new bonnet featuring a bigger hump, a new rear-view mirror, and it lost its lower lip in the radiator opening. Three months later, after the victory in Kristianstad, the Maserati team was in Venezuela, with only three points separating the Italian contenders (Ferrari 28 points versus Maserati 25 points). The two Works 450Ss seen in Sweden were entered at Caracas for the Venezuelan GP on November 3, 1957. The old warrior #4503 with race number 2 was registered for Jean Behra and Harry Schell while the younger #4507 with race number 4 was entered for Stirling Moss and Tony Brooks who was part of the Maserati team with the permission of Aston Martin. Fangio, who had influenza, was not seen in Venezuela. At the end of the practice session, both 450Ss had secured best times. Maserati had big hopes.

For the race, Behra had a mediocre start with #4503, but soon the French driver was in first place while Moss in #4507, who had overtaken 25 cars during his first lap, was on the hunt. After the first third of the race, the 450Ss were leading and Maserati race director Ugolini told his drivers to slow down, since he had told all drivers that their cars had already been sold to South American customers. Then the nightmare began for Maserati. At high speed, Moss crashed his #4507 in lap 32 while he was overtaking a slow AC Bristol which had drifted into his path. The impact was terrible. Then Moss ran to the pits, where Behra's car #4503 was refueling.

Journalist Hans Tanner, who acted as Temple Buell's race manager (see the #4508 chapter), later reported: "...Guerino Bertocchi, the chief mechanic, pulled the pressure hose out of the gas tank and Ugolini yelled "GO" to Behra. As Behra hit the starter button there was a dull explosion and a belch of flame at the rear of the car burning gas was spewing out of the pressure hose. Bertocchi tried to

smother the flaming hose with his arms while Behra, his clothes ablaze, vaulted out of the car, falling heavily on the concrete pit apron. People were running in all directions, but the fire squad had the fire out almost as suddenly as it had started..." Behra's hands were badly burned, so Moss hopped into the seat and drove off. He hopped out of the seat almost as quickly, for it was one part of the burning car that the firemen had neglected! He endured a lap then came in ... painfully burned... and Harry Schell then inherited the "hot seat."

Schell went off and started gaining time over the Ferraris. Despite its previous setback, the Maserati was still the fastest car on the track. Disaster came in lap 55 when just as #4503 overtook Bonnier's 300S, the latter blew a rear tire, hit the 450S then a lamppost. The 450S went out of control and crashed into a stone wall. Its fuel tank blew up and the car was immediately in a blast of flames. Local firemen tried to extinguish the fire, but it was too late for #4503. Miraculously, Bonnier and Schell escaped, slightly injured but alive. Incredulously, they watched Maserati's last hope go up in flames. Added to severe financial difficulties, this disaster tolled the bell for Maserati.

For a long time, it was not known, what had happened to either car after the disaster in Caracas. All the damaged works cars returned to Italy and a different fate followed for both 450S in Venezuela: #4503, which was destroyed by the inextinguishable flames, was scrapped by the factory in Modena, while #4507 which was severely crashed on the front but not destroyed, was rebuilt and started a new life in South America and much later in the USA but with a different chassis number (see 4507 chapter).

But the glorious winning car from Sebring in 1957 no longer exists.

When Harry Schell was hit by Jo Bonnier's Maserati 300S, #4503 was thrown against a stone wall. The impact was so strong that the fuel tank burst, and the car was a ball of fire. Firemen finally extinguished the flames, watched by hundreds of spectators on the wall above, but the car was a total loss and never saw another racetrack again. It was the end for #4503. *(Walter Bäumer Collection)*

4503 RACE HISTORY

20	Jan.	1957	1,000 km Buenos Aires	Juan Manuel Fangio/Stirling Moss (no. 2) DNF
23	March	1957	12 Hours of Sebring, Florida	Juan Manuel Fangio/Jean Behra (no. 19) 1.OA
11	May	1957	Mille Miglia	Jean Behra, DNS, crashed in testing
26	May	1957	Nürburgring 1,000 kms	Harry Schell/Hans Herrmann/Juan Manuel Fangio/Stirling Moss (no. 2) DNF
22	June	1957	24 Hours of Le Mans	Jean Behra/André Simon (no. 2) DNF
30	June	1957	Race of the Two Worlds, Monza	Jean Behra (no. 10) DNS
11	Aug.	1957	Swedish GP, Kristianstad	Stirling Moss/Harry Schell (no. 8) DNF
03	Nov.	1957	Venezuela GP, Caracas	Jean Behra/Stirling Moss/Harry Schell (no. 2) DNF, crash

4504

Completed: May 22, 1957
Engine: #4504.
Engine capacity: 4.5 Liter
Color: Red

Jim Kimberly was the CEO of the Kimberly-Clark paper company based at 919, North Michigan Avenue in Chicago, Illinois. He was tall, good-looking man with silver hair. His nickname was "Gentleman Jim", and he was, in the early 1950s the President of the Sports Car Club of America (SCCA). Kimberly had bought several Ferraris, among them, two of the big 375MMs, two 340 Americas, a 121LM and a 625LM.

He also became a Maserati customer and had purchased a 200Si, chassis number #2412. He was told about the huge power of the 450S that was unrolled in January 1957 in Buenos Aires and so he wanted one of the new V8s. Kimberly contacted the factory in Modena directly on March 11, 1957, and placed his order. He participated with his 200Si in the 12 Hours of Sebring in Florida on March 24, 1957, where he saw Juan Manuel Fangio's and Jean Behra's dominance over Ferrari with their 450S (see the 4503 chapter). He was confident that he would get a mighty weapon from Modena for his further race activities.

Kimberly's car, #4504, was completed on May 22 and shipped to Chicago on May 29. It became the first 450S to be privately owned and raced in the USA. During Kimberly's ownership, the car was not used extensively. He took his new toy with race number 115 to the Road America race in Wisconsin on June 23, 1957. During the race, steering problems occurred, and he was overtaken by smaller cars, crossing the finish line in sixth place.

Kimberly had entered his car for the Road America race on September 8, but instead he drove his smaller 200Si because the 450S main transmission mount bolt sheared twice in practice. Also, the car did not appear for the race in Nassau, Bahamas, that was scheduled for December 1957.

On January 11, 1958, Kimberly had entered his 'Big Maserati' in the First Annual Orange Bowl National Championship Sports Car Races in Opa Locka, Florida, but the car did not arrive, and his owner preferred to drive his smaller 200Si but did not see the finish. Kimberly realized that he did not like the big Maserati, but he took it to Cuba for the Grand Prix that was driven on public roads through Havana on February 24, 1958. This event saw a very strong field

of competitors like Moss, Fangio, Shelby, Behra, von Trips, Hill, Gregory, and others, attracted by the huge prize money the organizers had announced. Kimberly had plans to drive his 200Si in Cuba, but he had crashed the car near his winter home in Palm Springs and although new parts were ordered from Maserati, it could not be repaired in time for the race in Havana.

Joel Finn wrote in his book *Caribbean Capers* about the races in Cuba: "Kimberly made the reluctant decision to switch to his 450S. The 450S, which Kimberly never liked driving, had just been completely rebuilt mechanically, and it was for sale. Kimberly's unexpected switch to the 450S caused a good deal of confusion with the race organizers in Havana, as they had no advance warning regarding the change in plans…"

Temple Buell had hired Fangio to race his 450S (see the #4508 chapter) and had previously ordered parts and a new engine from Italy. Not sure if the package would arrive in time, Marcello Giambertone, Fangio's manager, negotiated a tentative deal with Jim Kimberly to rent his 450S for Fangio to race it in Cuba if they could not get the new engine for Buell's car in time. But the engine for Temple Buell's car arrived and so Kimberly needed to engage a driver for his car.

Joel Finn: "Jim Kimberly did not like the circuit, thinking it was dangerous and slippery. This made him very uncomfortable in his Maserati 450S at speed, and he motored around the whole session slowly in comparison to the other powerful Maseratis and Ferraris. Even though he was not pushing his car to the limit, Kimberly managed to jump a curb near the Parque Maceo, which spooked him even further. Maurice Trintignant tried out Kimberly's car later in the session and didn't like it at all. He felt it was unstable in the corners, possibly due to some damage resulting from Kimberly's curb-climbing incident. This report did nothing to improve Kimberly's confidence in the 450S and his rapidly waning desire to drive any further that weekend.

"Influencing Kimberly's attitude toward the race was a contretemps regarding the status of his relief driver, Harold "Hal" Ullrich of Evanston, Illinois. On Friday, when Ullrich signed in at the Hotel Lincoln, it was discovered that his FIA

OPPOSITE: Jim Kimberly was a handsome man and President of the Sports Car Club of America (SCCA). He was a former Ferrari and a Maserati customer and became the owner of #4504. But this car did not make him happy. *(Laird Scott)*

Kimberly intended to race his 450S with race number 5, but ultimately decided to field his smaller Maserati 200Si with the same number and #4504 received a new race number, 115. *(Dyke Ridgley Collection)*

A rare color shot from Elkhart Lake. #4504 had just been delivered from the factory and it became obvious that Kimberly was not comfortable driving the car. *(Walter Bäumer Collection)*

Jim Kimberly in the seat of his 450S while his mechanics are working on it. Note the big rear-view mirror. *(Laird Scott)*

#4504 with heavily taped lights in the pits during the practice sessions for the 1958 Cuba GP. The car had been crashed by its owner during practice who had difficulties with the circuit. Behind the wheel is Maurice Trintignant who drove some laps but did not like the car. Jim Kimberly stands on the far left of the photograph. *(Klemantaski Collection)*

Jim Kimberly gets advice from one of the officials during practice for the Cuban GP. *(Bernard Cahier Archives)*

125

Alfredo Momo on the far left and his mechanic Andy Samariti are freezing while watching Stirling Moss test #4504 at Bridgehampton in February 1958. Soon, both Moss and the car were on their way to the warmer Bahamas. *(Henry Tredwell)*

Crawford powers #4504 round a corner at Nassau in December 1958. Note the cap that was mounted just over the opening for the exhaust pipes behind the front wheel arch. *(Bill Cummings Collection)*

Another photograph of the Don Perkins car with Crawford during the 1959 Nassau Speed Week. Its driver could really handle the car. *(Terry O'Neil Collection)*

Owner Don Perkins entered #4504 with his mechanic and driver Hal Ullrich in the Pomona races early in March 1959. This is the opening lap with Ullrich followed by Maurice Trintignant in the Cooper/Climax (no. 83) and the Porsche 550 of Joe Playan (no. 29). *(Walter Bäumer Collection)*

Bill Krause handled his battered #4502 magnificently and outgunned Hal Ullrich in #4504 at Pomona, in March 1959. *(Walter Bäumer Collection)*

OPPOSITE: Steering problems gave Hal Ullrich an early retirement in the car's last competition race at Pomona. *(Walter Bäumer Collection)*

competition driver's license had expired. Ullrich claimed he had renewed it but had not yet received the license in the mail from the FIA. The CSC sent a cablegram to the FIA to clarify the matter, but it was already after normal business hours in Paris and the office had closed for the weekend, so no answer was forthcoming. The CSC decided that Ullrich could not drive until the matter was resolved. During the Sunday practice, Ullrich snuck out in the 450S for a few laps to learn the circuit. When he returned to the pit area, a marshal realized it was not Kimberly in the car and reported the transgression to Race Control. This led to a stern warning from Race Control that if Ullrich attempted to drive again, Kimberly and his 450S would be disqualified from the race."

So, Kimberly had to do the job himself and finished a disappointing fifteenth, beaten not only by the big cars of Moss, the winner, Gregory and Shelby but also by no less than three of the smaller, much less powerful 200Ss.

Kimberly placed a for sale advertisement for the car in the *Sports Cars Newsletter* in the issue dated March 31, 1958, but without giving a price. As this seemed to be unsuccessful, he offered his 200Si and the big Maserati through Chicago dealer Harry Woodnorth in May 1958, who asked US$12,500 for the #4504 including spares.

The car was sold to Harry Rollings, a medical doctor from Savannah, Georgia, who had previously raced a Jaguar D-Type. His first race entry was at Walterboro in South Carolina in the Carnival of Speed event on July 4-5, 1958. In the drag race over a quarter mile, Rollings came first, but in race 3, the Combahee Trophy, Rollings was beaten by Ed Rahal in Rollings ex-D-Type in very wet weather conditions. Italian cars are not made for the rain.

In race 5, Rollings did not finish as the car suffered from misfiring because of a wet ignition. After the race, Rollings parted with the car. It was transported to Ed Crawford's shop in Northfield, Illinois, and finally sold to Don Perkins of Winnetka, Illinois. Perkins did not pay for the car until early in October 1958.

After the payment arrived, the car was prepared in haste to get it to the Virginia International Raceway, Danville on October 5, 1958. Its driver was John Haas, a young and talented amateur who worked for a car dealership in Illinois, but in the race, Haas had problems braking the big car and left the road on his first lap. Perkins was not satisfied with the poor presentation of his car by Ed Crawford's mechanic and changed to Hal Ullrich.

Perkins entered Ed Crawford with his 450S in the Nassau Speed Week in the Bahamas from November 30 to December 7, 1958. Stirling Moss, on his way to the Bahamas for a holiday with his wife Katie and his sister Pat, stopped in Bridgehampton one week before the race and tested #4504, which was now in the very experienced hands of Alfredo Momo's mechanics in his shop in New York who had sorted the car for Perkins before embarking to Nassau.

After much rain in the first few days, Crawford had to get used to the car and finished fourth after 5 laps in the sprint race. In the Governor's Trophy, he was third on the podium after 25 laps, beating the new race-superstars Pedro and

Ricardo Rodriguez in their Ferrari 250TR and Porsche 550. During the Memorial Trophy, with only five cars entered, Crawford battled with E. D. Martin in his powerful 3-liter Ferrari 250TR. The Ferrari won after 12 laps with Crawford second. In the Nassau Trophy race over 56 laps, four Maseratis were entered, among them two other 450S (see the #4506 and #4508 chapters). Crawford had a bad start but gained speed. He was fighting with his big Maserati to keep on the road and finished fourth, the only Maserati in the field.

The new 1959 season started for #4504 on February 15 in Fort Worth, Texas, for the 5th Annual Frostbite Races on the Eagle Mountain airfield circuit. Hal Ullrich, who was there as mechanic and driver, finished third in class in race 4 won by the Maserati 300S-Chevy of Ebb Rose and second in class in race 8 won by the 250S of Gary Laughlin.

Then in Pomona, California on March 7 for the Examiner GP, Don Perkins again trusted Hal Ullrich to handle #4504 driving against three other 450S (see the #4502, #4506 and #4509 chapters). In race 6 over 10 laps, Ullrich finished an unremarkable twentieth, while Bill Krause was the happy winner in #4502 in front of 40,000 visitors. In the early stages of race 11, the main race that weekend, #4504 developed the usual steering problems and was out of the race. This was Hal Ullrich's last ride in this car, which was also retired from racing. Later, #4504 was more or less dismantled, its engine removed and installed in a speed boat project that finally ended up in Florida, and a big Ford engine was placed in the chassis. It might be possible that the dealer C. R. Berry Sales offered the car in the *Miami Herald* in its October 1960 issue.

The car lost the rear section of its coachwork for unknown reasons, and it was then sold as a rolling chassis to Simeon Shortman from Massachusetts in 1967. In the meantime, Joel Finn from New York had acquired the original motor from #4504 in Florida. He contacted Shortman to sell try to purchase the car, but the negotiations came to an end when Shortman found out that Finn had bought the original motor.

In August 1979, he finally sold the chassis to Finn in exchange for a Lotus 19. One year later, the chassis, body and engine were sold to Virgil Milette in New York. After some years of ownership, Milette sold the 450S to dealer Steve Forristall from Texas. He copied this car to build a replica with the number "4505." In 1987, #4504 was back in its Italian homeland, and owned by Luigi Mancini. He commissioned a full restoration in the same year. Broker Keith Duly managed the subsequent sale of the car to Maserati collector, Alfredo Brenner from Houston, Texas. It was restored again and sold to a prominent American amateur racer in Arkansas. The car had received a new front and rear end, while the mid-section remained original. Today, #4504 resides in a great Ferrari and Maserati collection.

OPPOSITE: The current and long time owner of #4504 hard cornering at Laguna Seca in 2013. *(Peter Singhoff)*

4504 RACE HISTORY

23	June	1957	Road America, Wisconsin, race 4	Jim Kimberly (no. 115) 6.OA
24	Feb.	1958	Cuba GP, Havana	Jim Kimberly (no. 44) 15.OA
04	July	1958	Walterboro, South Carolina, drag race	Harry Rollings (no. 40) 1.OA
05	July	1958	Walterboro, South Carolina, race 3	Harry Rollings (no. 40) 2.OA
05	July	1958	Walterboro, South Carolina, race 5	Harry Rollings (no. 40) DNF
05	Oct.	1958	Danville, Virginia	John Haas (no. 9) DNF
05	Dec.	1958	Governor's Trophy, Nassau, Bahamas, heat 1	Ed Crawford (no. 7) 4.OA – 3.i.C
05	Dec.	1958	Governor's Trophy, Nassau, Bahamas, heat 2	Ed Crawford (no. 7) 3.OA – 2.i.C.
07	Dec.	1958	Memorial Trophy, Nassau, Bahamas	Ed Crawford (no. 7) 2.OA – 1.i.C.
07	Dec.	1958	Nassau Trophy, Nassau, Bahamas	Ed Crawford (no. 7) 4.OA – 2.i.C.
15	Feb.	1959	Frostbite Races, Fort Worth, Texas, race 4	Hal Ullrich (no. 7) 3.i.C.
15	Feb.	1959	Frostbite Races, Fort Worth, Texas, race 8	Hal Ullrich (no. 7) 2.i.C.
07	March	1959	Pomona, California, race 6	Hal Ullrich (no. 171) 20.OA
08	March	1959	Examiner GP, Pomona, California	Hal Ullrich (no. 171) DNF

4505 later renumbered #4506

OPPOSITE: All the Maserati mechanics are listening carefully when Stirling Moss explains what he wants with #4505 during its manufacture, when the car was in bare metal. *(Walter Bäumer Collection)*

Completed: May 8, 1957
Engine: #4505
Engine capacity: 4.5 Liter
Color: Red

#4505 was the fifth car built in the 450S series. A significant trademark of this car were the two big nostrils on each side of the radiator opening to improve brake cooling. No headrest was behind the driver.

The car began its short and disappointing sporting career in the 1957 Mille Miglia. The day before the race, Jean Behra, who was scheduled to start the Mille Miglia with another factory 450S (see the #4503 chapter) had a serious accident hitting a truck at high speed during an open road test, which sent him to the hospital and the 450S to the factory for a complete rebuild.

Therefore, the only 450S available, #4505, made the last start of the race in the early hours of May 11 at 5:37 a.m. with Stirling Moss behind the wheel and his trusted co-driver from 1955 and 1956, Denis Jenkinson as his teammate. They had tested the car the day before on some sections of the route and timed its acceleration from 12 to 93 mph in just 6 seconds! Moss later wrote in his book *My Cars, My Career*: "…the car had an extra two-speed gearbox just behind the clutch, the 450's standard gearbox, of course, being mounted at the rear. The idea was that using this device we could run with an extra high-speed set of ratios to Pescara, then I could select 'low' for the mountain section to Bologna, and then 'high' again back to Brescia, changing normally on the main gearbox all the time. But I had discovered that this intermediate two-speed box would change beautifully on the move, so we intended to swap around as necessary all the way…." The two men were confident, and everybody saw them among the favorites for victory.

Moss: "…we were hardly out of Brescia itself before we were up into high ratio fifth and the rev counter needle was hovering on 7,600 rpm, which was near as dammit 180mph, and we couldn't help grinning at each other. It was a fantastic experience."

But disaster struck! After about three and a half minutes in the race, traveling at about 145 mph, Moss pushed the brakes when going into a tight left hander and the car slowed. Moss: "Then my foot suddenly banged down to the floorboards and the car leapt forward as the brakes were released. The brake pedal had just snapped off."

The car finally came to a halt but was out of the biggest Italian sports car event. #4505 with both drivers was pushed back by spectators to the starting line in Brescia, surrounded by the crowd of dumbfounded *Tifosi*, a common Italian term for race enthusiasts. The Maserati team had already packed all the tools to go to the next checkpoint. Completely amazed, they saw their leading driver arrive back at the starting point in the car they had expected to win. Many years later, Moss told one of the authors that some mechanics were on their knees in tears.

Finally, the courageous Giorgio Scarlatti saved the honor of Maserati with his fourth-place finish in a 300S. The last and tragic Mille Miglia held in 1957 was won by veteran Piero Taruffi in a Ferrari.

Later Denis Jenkinson wrote in his report about the Mille Miglia for the UK magazine Motor Sport: "Had such a breakage occurred on a British car there would have been harsh words and rudery in the Press, as it was an Italian car there was some pretty lurid shouting and yelling, but most people, including ourselves, were almost speechless. The reason for such a stupid failure on a brand-new car was hard to justify and can only be blamed on a flaw in the metal tube that forms the brake-pedal arm. Even so it was completely and utterly inexcusable, for closer study showed that it had started to fail at least two days before the race, but though we were annoyed about the whole affair we had to commiserate with Maserati for they had put everything they had into this 4½-litre and for the first time ever there had been a good certainty of a Maserati win in the Mille Miglia, a thing that has not yet happened, for that "four-five" is a fabulous performer."

Despite the disappointing result of the 450S in the Mille Miglia, everybody at Maserati nevertheless remained confident for the rest of the Sportscar Championship, especially since the Maserati team was second behind Ferrari by just two points in the aggregate of the first three events, with 17 points for Maserati against 19 points for Ferrari.

It was, therefore, a highly motivated team that found itself in Germany at the Nürburgring on May 26, 1957, to compete in the 1,000 km where two Maserati

#4505 in dark primer but without its engine. Some details like the nostrils on the openings for brake cooling and one of the air intakes on top of its front fenders were added at the last moment before it was painted. *(Klemantaski Collection)*

OPPOSITE: Now the car is finished and ready to be pushed outside the factory for taking some photographs before going to Brescia for the 1957 Mille Miglia. *(Unknown photographer)*

OPPOSITE: #4505, sponsored by Italian pasta company Buitoni, at Piazza Vittoria in Brescia the day before the start of the Mille Miglia. Everybody thought that this was the winning car of the legendary 1,000 miles race. *(Klemantaski Collection)*

The car in Brescia with Moss and his trusted co-driver Denis Jenkinson. It received a lot of attention from the "Tifosi." *(Walter Bäumer Collection)*

OPPOSITE: In the early morning of May 11, 1957, #4505 with Moss and Jenkinson on the famous ramp in Brescia and ready for the legendary Mille Miglia. All hopes were high. *(Walter Bäumer Collection)*

"Push in this direction" says co-driver Denis Jenkinson as all hope had disappeared after a few miles of driving when the brake pedal broke, and the car was pushed back to Brescia by a huge crowd of spectators. It was an emotional disaster for the entire Maserati crew. *(Walter Bäumer Collection)*

Chassis #4505 is unloaded from the transport truck shortly after arriving at the Nürburgring paddock for the 1,000km race. *(Klemantaski Collection)*

OPPOSITE: #4505 prepared in the pits of the Nürburgring in Germany for the 1,000 km race two weeks after the Mille Miglia. *(Walter Bäumer Collection)*

In the Mille Miglia, the brake pedal broke, and the car was withdrawn and at the race on the Nürburgring, the left, rear wheel flew off. Maserati made a great car but the maintenance for their cars was often very bad. *(Unknown photographer)*

...and he walked away! Moss had a lift back to the pits when his 450S lost its wheel. *(Walter Bäumer Collection)*

450S were entered: #4505 for Fangio and Moss with race number 1, and #4503 for Schell and Herrmann with race number 2. Both cars were qualified by the great Juan Manuel Fangio in pole positions, ahead of the Aston Martin of Tony Brooks! Moss could not start his car and lost over one minute but caught Brooks after eight laps. Just entering the Schwalbenschwanz section, the hub shaft broke and the left rear wheel turned wildly, flying from the car. Again, #4505 was out of a race. An MG picked Moss up and drove him back to the pits from where he rejoined the race in #4503. But this car also failed later, and Moss and Fangio shared a 300S.

#4505, after two successive retirements for its first two races at the Mille Miglia and then at the Nürburgring seemed to have bad luck. But it was, above all, caused by a lack of preparation as often happened in the sporting history of Maserati in those years. The Nürburgring was the last entry for the car with its identity of #4505. The factory was now pressed for time, needing to fulfill John Edgar's order from the USA, and re-stamped the car to #4506. The next chapter, #4506, has the continuation story of one single car with two official chassis numbers.

OPPOSITE: Back in the pits, Moss took over a 300S and was back in the race, here passing his abandoned #4505. It was the car's last race with this identity. *(Klemantaski Collection)*

4505 RACE HISTORY

| 11 | May | 1957 | Mille Miglia | Stirling Moss/Denis Jenkinson (no. 537) DNF |
| 26 | May | 1957 | 1,000 Km Nürburgring | Juan Manuel Fangio/Stirling Moss (no. 1) DNF |

4506 ex #4505

Completed: June 18, 1957
Engine: #4506
Engine capacity: 4.5 Liter
Color: Red

After its first, rather unsuccessful life in Europe as a factory car (see chapter 4505), #4505 was given a makeover when it returned from the Nürburgring.

John Edgar, a wealthy entrepreneur from Encino, California, witnessed the impressive performance of Fangio and Behra at Sebring, where their 450S (see the #4503 chapter) steamrolled the entire Ferrari opposition.

His driver, Carroll Shelby, convinced him to change from Ferrari to Maserati and Edgar wanted the winning car. But Maserati refused as they had other plans to use this car themselves, so Edgar ordered a new 450S via Maserati race director, Nello Ugolini. In the meantime, the factory loaned him the 300S in which Stirling Moss was second at Sebring. John Edgar always operated in a first-class manner and his magnificent, polished aluminum truck that functioned simultaneously as race car transporter, machine shop, spare parts store and hospitality became famous.

Edgar was in a great hurry to receive the big Maserati. But in the meantime, the new #4506 being assembled for Edgar had been reassigned by the factory for the construction of the 450S Zagato-bodied coupé that Moss had requested for the next 24 Hours of Le Mans (see the #4501/4512 chapter)! Consequently, a makeover was undertaken on the used #4505 which was just back from the disappointing Nürburgring race. The two nostrils from the front were taken away, a profiled headrest was added, and the gearbox was changed. With new upholstery and fresh paint, voilá, the used #4505 became a "brand new" car, now labeled #4506, and invoiced as new for US$20,000 to John Edgar.

This change of chassis numbers was noted by enthusiast and collector Joel Finn from New York, who mentioned it in a feature for *Trident*, the magazine of the Maserati Club UK, in its 1977 winter issue. It was also reported by Luigi Orsini and Franco Zagari in their book Maserati – A complete History from 1926 to the present, published in 1980. Respected historian Willem Oosthoek uncovered more details in the late 1990s, confirming that #4505 and #4506 are one and the same car by asking the question: why did the 450S #4505 disappear from the radar after the Nürburgring race? Looking carefully at period photographs,

he noticed on the "two cars" the same lower lip on the radiator opening, the same counters on the dashboard, the same round air intakes on top of both front fenders, and the same tank cap cutouts on the rear bonnet; so many small features that are not found on any other 450S series car.

Papers in the factory archive confirm that Maserati shipped the "new" car on July 11, 1957 via Genoa harbor to Maserati Corporation of America (MCA) in New York where it arrived on July 18 and from there it was transported to its new owner in California.

#4506 continued its second life in the USA with John Edgar's favorite driver, the "farmer" from Texas, Carroll Shelby who debuted #4506 for the first time in the US on July 28, 1957, at Lime Rock, Connecticut and won its first race! On almost all the cars that Shelby drove, his lucky race number was 98. Shelby easily won both heats. In the second heat, the car was 20 seconds ahead of the Jaguar D-Type of Walt Hansgen who finished second. This success was followed by a second victory on August 4 at Danville, a fast circuit in Virginia. Shelby set the car in pole position and crossed the finish line as the winner. Shelby's master mechanic, Joe Landaker, had fitted a tell-tale tachometer on the dashboard and given his driver instructions never to exceed 6,000 rpm unless it was necessary to win a race. When he checked the tach at the completion of the race, it read 5,400 rpm, so clearly a great deal of power was left in reserve.

Stunned by this performance, the local newspaper *The Bee* later titled the headline: "Shelby's Maserati ran away…" After its misfortunes in Europe as #4505, #4506 is therefore starting its new American life very well!

At Montgomery in New York on August 18, the car was retired by Shelby due to a broken transmission directly after the start. Then came the race at Riverside, California on September 21. In his first lap during practice, Shelby crashed heavily, putting himself in the hospital.

He later remembered: "…My worst crash during my years of intensive racing occurred during the first meet at the then-new Riverside International Raceway on

Shelby guns #4506 around the track at Danville. The car showed its strength again and it was the second consecutive win for Shelby with the car. *(Walter Bäumer Collection)*

Shelby just back from winning the race in Danville. It seems that he had ruined the right leg of his striped bib overall during the drive. *(Walter Bäumer Collection)*

OPPOSITE: "Many thanks. Great to get the silverware, but where is the check for my prize money?" *(Walter Bäumer Collection)*

September 21, 1957. To make matters worse, I wasn't driving just some ordinary sports car, but a $20,000 Maserati belonging to my sponsor, John Edgar. This magnificent 4.5-liter machine was his pride and joy, and he didn't even have the satisfaction of seeing it complete a single lap at Riverside that day.

On the very first practice lap of this 3.27-mile rolling course, I pulled the biggest, costliest, and most unforgivable booboo of my entire racing career. It happened on Turn Six, where, I guess, I got just a bit too eager and self-important. The next thing that happened was that I wasn't driving the Maser anymore. It was driving me and going like a runaway steam engine – in a straight line – right into an earth bank at pretty close to 80 mph and there wasn't a thing in this world I could do. The front end had cashed out completely. I guess the term "explosion" would describe what happened rather than just an ordinary "collision." But for my seat belt, the chances are that I'd still be flying, probably in orbit. Turn Six, in those days, didn't have any guard rails and quite a bit of sand had begun to blow across the track even before the start of practice. That was a convenient and logical thing to blame. Anyway, I got two wheels in the sand and when I slammed on the brakes, the wheels didn't slow down at all. They simply locked while the car continued on its merry way. The collision was a tremendous jolt to my head and displaced the cartilage in my nose. I was so badly cut up that I must have blacked out completely for a few moments, I have no clear recollection of the impact itself."

Seventy-odd stitches were needed to put Shelby back together, but he promptly announced he would be ready to drive again at the next major race scheduled to take place at Palm Springs, California, on November 3rd. The 450S, however, was not so easily repaired.

A survey of the damage was undertaken, and the results were not encouraging. Besides the badly demolished left-front end, the tail, headrest, windshield, and hood all received some damage. The entire left-side front of the chassis was destroyed and needed replacement. New framing material was rush ordered from Modena, but they could not provide the pieces quickly. As Edgar and Shelby desired to run the car at Palm Springs, only a few weeks were available to repair this extensive damage. Magician Joe Landaker repaired the bent chassis, fitted a new front suspension and brake drum and hub assembly.

The engine had to be removed and repairs made to the block where the front motor mount had been torn out and then reassembled and reinstalled in the chassis. A new radiator and oil cooler were fitted. The clutch and transaxle were also rebuilt. Landaker then straightened all the body panels as well as he could in the time available. A new but smaller windshield was made. Except for the left-front fender which permanently retained a different line due to the accident, the rest of #4506 looked quite presentable. By working phenomenal hours, Landaker managed to have the car ready in time for a somewhat recovered Shelby to run at the Palm Springs airport course on November 2-3, 1957. The radiator was taped over against the cold and half the body was painted in black primer. Shelby made it again, finishing first in heat 1 ahead of John von Neumann in a Ferrari 500 and again in heat 2 beating Max Balchowsky in his 5.4-liter Old Yeller.

Before the race in Montgomery in August 1957. Chassis #4506 has just been unloaded in the paddock and Carroll Shelby reverses it alongside two Mercedes 300SLs. *(Revs Institute)*

In August 1957 before going to Elkhart Lake, Carroll Shelby and his future wife, Jan Harrison are posing beside the car in front of John Edgar's residence in Encino, California. #4506 with it round race number 8 was planned for Elkhart lake in September were the car went but did not race. Instead Shelby drove there a 300S. *(Will Edgar Motorsport Archive)*

The car was also used to get a good seat in a
restaurant in Los Angeles *(Unknown photographer)*

Then back to Riverside for the races on November 16-17, where Shelby and #4506 had a strong opponent on the grid: Masten Gregory in the Temple Buell-owned 450S that had a stronger engine fitted (see the #4508 chapter). On the first day, Shelby was beaten by Gregory who took first place but on the second day it was Shelby who earned the silverware with Gregory in third, beaten by Dan Gurney in the 4.9-liter Ferrari owned by Frank Arciero. In that race, Shelby had lost the lead and was sixth. The "chicken-farmer" drove like hell in front of 20,000 spectators and caught up 22 seconds to the leading car, and on lap 17, Gregory saw the open exhausts of #4506! It was a crowd-pleasing win for Shelby.

In December 1957, the Bahamas Speed Week was an important event organized by the FIA, where stars like Stirling Moss, Peter Collins, Ricardo Rodriguez and Jo Bonnier participated. Carroll Shelby, with the #4506 equipped with two small additional headlights mounted on its upper front just besides the fenders and a third on the lower lip of the radiator opening for the tropical twilight, could not enter the first race due to missing spare parts that had been stuck at the Nassau customs. The problems were cleared and #4506 was ready to battle against the Temple Buell 450S, again with Masten Gregory behind its wheel who had been first in the Tourist Trophy. The sprint race was won by Phil Hill in a big Ferrari 335S. Shelby in #4506 followed in second with Gregory in the blue and white #4508 was third. But the main race of the week, the Nassau Trophy, saw a very strong entry field. Stirling Moss who gunned in a Ferrari 290MM, was on top of the podium with Shelby a fine second place and Phil Hill as third.

After the Nassau event, #4506 was shipped to Florida, where it was stored at the Rolls-Royce and Cadillac dealer Charlie Berry at 2185, N.W. 27th Avenue in Miami. Willem Oosthoek and Michel Bollée reported in their book about the Maserati 450S "...When Berry was invited to display the Maserati at a car show at the Keys Coliseum, he asked Miami based mechanic Lee Lilley for a trailer to move the car. Lilley had a better idea. Through his contacts with the Miami

police, he was assigned two officers on motorcycles to escort him and the 4.5 on the eight miles of public road to the Coliseum. In 2004, Lilley still remembered how the car belched fire from its exhaust pipes on the trip."

For the new 1958 season, John Edgar had a large yellow triangle painted on the nose and around the radiator opening of his #4506 and still retained his confidence in Carroll Shelby, who started the new season in February in another FIA event, the Cuban GP contested in the streets of Havana on February 24, 1958.

US-Ferrari importer Luigi Chinetti, who was involved in the organization of the race in Cuba, wired a telegram to John Edgar on January 15, 1958, and confirmed the starting money of US$2,000 for the 450S. The high prize money attracted numerous teams and drivers to travel to the Caribbean. It saw a very strong field of competitors, among them two other 450S (see the #4504 and #4508 chapters) and six smaller Maserati. Shelby brought the 450S to third place in a race that was stopped prematurely following the exit from the track by a privately owned Ferrari into the crowd of spectators, tragically causing many victims! Stirling Moss and Masten Gregory finished first and second in their Ferraris.

From sunny Cuba back to California where Shelby in #4506 won the Palm Springs sprint race on April 12 but the car did not start on the next day because of brake problems. The Palm Springs event was the last participation by Carroll Shelby in John Edgar's #4506. Shelby then tried his luck in Formula 1 in Europe in a private Maserati 250F from Scuderia Centro Sud and started at the French GP in Reims on July 6, 1958.

John Edgar then hired the promising young Dan Gurney who mastered the powerful 450S well with beautiful, controlled slides on the runways of the Tracy airport in California but had to retire from the lead just before the last lap because of a burst tire. Pete Woods next took over #4506, which received a new

OPPOSITE: #4506 was severely damaged. It was repaired in haste, and many years later, it was discovered that the front part of the chassis was not straight. (Will Edgar Motorsport Archive)

After the Riverside crash, Edgar's #4506 was repaired but partially unpainted and shipped to Palm Springs in primer only in November 1957. Shelby had recovered very well from the shock of his accident and won the race. (Jean-François Blachette Collection)

This blurry photograph shows the Edgar 450S in Nassau in 1957. To see the road during night driving, Joe Landaker had mounted two additional headlamps just beside the front fenders and a third one on the lower lip of the radiator opening. *(Sports Car)*

OPPOSITE: A quiet day at the Shelby-Hall dealership in Dallas. #4506 waits in the background beside the Ferrari 500TRC and 290MM, both owned by Temple Buell. Close to the camera is the white Maserati 200Si with blue stripes owned by Lance Reventlow *(Walter Bäumer Collection)*

No parking ticket for Shelby and #4506 at the 1958 Cuba GP. The front end of the car had been painted in yellow. The race took place under very poor safety conditions with full grandstands and crowds right next to the track. *(Bernard Cahier Archives)*

Flagger Al Torres jumps Carroll Shelby to the finish line as winner in the Palm Springs pre-race in April 1958. Carroll drove the #4506 car so hard for victory that he destroyed the brakes and was unable to use the 450S in the main race the next day as he drove the Edgar team's well-used backup Ferrari 410 Sport. *(Will Edgar Motorsport Archive)*

Now with a chromed race number and front nose tape, #4506 appeared at Riverside in June 1958 with driver Pete Woods. *(Walter Bäumer Collection)*

OPPOSITE: The big Pontiac race engine in #4506. The car received a lot of attention when it was at Riverside, in October 1958, now for Jim Rathmann. The combination of the Italian car and the powerful US-V8 turned out to be unsuccessful. The tachometer that Landaker had mounted on the dash is still there. *(Unknown photographer)*

The beat goes on with cheerleaders! #4506 under preparation for the race in Daytona in April 1959 *(FORD Museum / Dave Friedman)*

Chuck Daigh, who had retired his Ferrari at Daytona, took over #4506 from Jim Rathmann. He looks skeptical about the tachometer on the dash. The car had hit something, and later, it was retired with a blown engine. *(FORD Museum / Dave Friedman)*

paint job with a chrome nose decoration and numbers for the race on June 29, 1958, at Riverside. He finished sixth overall in race 7 but in race 12, it was another DNF, because the engine broke after ingesting sand in its carburetors during a too wide spin off the track. Edgar then changed the Maserati V8 engine for a big experimental Pontiac 6.3-liter V8 version whose carburetor pipes protruded from the bonnet which was largely cut for the occasion.

The Miami Herald wrote in its November 9, 1958, issue: "The engine in John Edgar's 5.7 Pontiac-Maserati isn't exactly what you'd find under the hood of a Pontiac parked on the street. It's one of six special engines Firestone had General Motors turn out for installation in the tire-test car at Indianapolis…" Landaker retained the original motor mounts, and all the under-hood sheet metal and frame structure remained as original to facilitate easy re-installation of the Maserati engine. The carburetor pipes were protected by the small windshield that was installed after Shelby's crash at Riverside. The car looked somewhat strange. Edgar had planned to entrust the wheel to Jim Rathmann, the winner of the Two Worlds race at Monza that June, for the highly contested and challenging Times GP at Riverside on October 12, but he was not satisfied with the handling of the car. On race day, #4506 did not take the start because the V8 Pontiac engine, missing water in the radiator, seized during the test drive with Jo Bonnier at the wheel.

#4506 was at this moment very tired; John Edgar in addition to the repair of the engine took the opportunity to restore the bodywork, which lost its small round air intakes on the front fenders, removed its small Maserati logo on the nose and installed a new grille with a large mesh and a new race number 68. The refreshed #4506 in full red appeared in December 1958 in Nassau for the Bahamas Speed Week organized under the FIA banner. Jim Rathmann retired again during the Nassau Trophy race, with a broken head gasket caused by a too-low water level in its radiator.

Edgar persevered and entered his 450S Pontiac in the 1,000 km of Daytona in Florida on April 5, 1959, again with Jim Rathmann who teamed up for this endurance race with Californian Chuck Daigh. Again, another retirement: the engine exploded after Daigh took over from Rathmann for only 11 laps in total on the oval. The transplant of the Pontiac engine on the Maserati chassis obviously was not satisfactory and Edgar, who was not discouraged by this failure, repatriated his 450S to Los Angeles. In April 1959, #4506 was seen on the cover of American car magazine *Speed Age*.

Edgar had ordered a new 520hp Maserati engine from the factory to be installed in his car. Modena sent him a V8 Marine version of 5.7-liter capacity, numbered #4513. The escalation of power continued! A bonnet with a bigger bump was fitted to accommodate the big Webers and the rear Borrani wire wheels, too fragile to withstand the engine torque, were replaced by Halibrands. But the new monstrous Motor from Modena came too late to be installed in time for the scheduled Kiwanis GP at Riverside. Chuck Daigh remembered in an

OPPOSITE: A scenic photograph of Chuck Daigh racing #4506 at Riverside in October 1959. The Pontiac engine was removed, and the car now had a beefy 5.7-liter Maserati boat engine installed. *(Jean-François Blachette Collection)*

interview in 2001 about the engine: "...I could not believe that the factory had not balanced it. Maybe the Italians didn't have heavy metal in those days. We had to put three big one-inch slugs of heavy metal in each counterweight to get it balanced, something that was very new at the time...."

#4506 competed very well in practice for its last two races with Chuck Daigh seated behind the wheel: in Santa Barbara on September 6, 1959, and then at Riverside for the Times GP on October 11. But unfortunately, it did not finish either of the races due to the broken transmission which did not support the torque of the big Maserati 5.7-liter engine!

Now John Edgar had had enough and ended the sporting career of his 450S, which had not shone in Europe in its first life as #4505 with Stirling Moss, but, on the other hand, met with success in the USA driven by Carroll Shelby as #4506 with five races won in 1957. Subsequent events showed that the Pontiac engine was unreliable, and the Maserati marine engine had too much torque. The car remained unused in Edgar's possession for a while until it was sold to an unknown person in California. Later #4506 was purchased by Joel Finn. Ex-restorer, Stephen Griswold, from Berkeley, California told one of the authors early in 2023: "In 1970, a transporter arrived at my door from Joel Finn. Subsequently, two beautiful cars were unloaded, a Maserati 450S #4506 and a Ferrari 410 Sport [...]. I discussed the work required with Joel and he gave his OK to start the job on the Maserati 450S. The car was missing its original engine and Joel had bought a marine unit used for hydroplane racing from Roberto Orsi, son of Maserati past factory owner Omar Orsi. This was an engine with a displacement of 6.4 liters. Externally, it was identical to the original. [...] When we disassembled the car, it was discovered that the frame

had been hit and repaired on the left front corner, following Shelby's crash Shelby at Riverside. We took accurate measurements from the right-hand side and used these to check the damaged area. Fortunately, we did this, because a discrepancy of one inch in length was discovered and a camber angle that also needed correcting. The car had been raced for many years like this! To fix these badly done repairs, we mounted the frame on our chassis table and repaired the damaged tubes. The final checks revealed that the car was now square, and the front-end geometry was equal side to side. The car was very complete. It had been parked after its engine had blown up, so it was in the same condition as it was when it finished its last race."

Peter Kaus from Frankfurt, Germany, wanted a 450S for his huge sports car collection, "Rosso Bianco", located in his museum in Aschaffenburg, near his hometown. Around 1973, he contacted Joel Finn and made an offer the American could not resist, and the car was back in Europe. It was tested by Willie Green on the Silverstone track in 1984 for a report published in the August issue of Classic & Sports Car.

Kaus entered it in the 1984 Mille Miglia Storica with Stephen Griswold as co-driver and raced it at two consecutive Oldtimer GP events on the Nürburgring in 1986 and 1987. On April 18, 1991, Peter Kaus sold the 450S to the banker Dr. Thomas Bscher from Cologne, Germany, who was a great Maserati fan and active amateur race driver. He used the car successfully in many historic race events in Europe. Dr. Bscher kept it for more than twenty years. Upon his retirement from racing, he finally sold #4506 in the beginning of 2017 to a new owner in Germany who, together with his brother, hosts the biggest Maserati race car collection worldwide. It was then cosmetically restored, and Shelby's yellow triangle added on the front.

4506 RACE HISTORY

28	July	1957	Lime Rock, Connecticut, SCCA Regional	Carroll Shelby (no. 138) 1.OA
04	Aug.	1957	Danville, Virginia, SCCA National	Carroll Shelby (no. 98) 1.OA
18	Aug.	1957	Montgomery, New York, SCCA National	Carroll Shelby (no. 8) DNF
21	Sept.	1957	Riverside, California	Carroll Shelby (no. 98) DNS, crash in practice
03	Nov.	1957	Palm Springs, California	Carroll Shelby (no. 98) 1.OA
17	Nov.	1957	Riverside, California	Carroll Shelby (no. 98) 1.OA
06	Dec.	1957	Governor's Trophy, Nassau, Bahamas	Carroll Shelby (no. 98) 3.OA
08	Dec.	1957	Intl. Trophy, Nassau, Bahamas	Carroll Shelby (no. 98) 2.OA
24	Feb.	1958	Cuba GP, Havana	Carroll Shelby (no. 6) 3.OA
12	April	1958	Palm Springs, California, sprint race	Carroll Shelby (no. 98) 1.OA
11	May	1958	Tracy, California	Dan Gurney (no. 198) DNF
29	June	1958	Riverside, California	Pete Woods (no. 98) DNF
12	Oct.	1958	Times GP, Riverside, California	Jim Rathmann (no. 98) DNS
07	Dec.	1958	Intl. Trophy, Nassau, Bahamas	Jim Rathmann (no. 68) DNF
05	April	1959	Daytona, Florida	Jim Rathmann/Chuck Daigh (no. 68) DNF
19	July	1959	Kiwanis GP, Riverside, California	Chuck Daigh (no. 98) DNS
06	Sept.	1959	Santa Barbara, California	Chuck Daigh (no. 98) DNF
11	Oct.	1959	Times GP, Riverside, California	Chuck Daigh (no. 98) DNF

4507

Completed: July 30, 1957
Engine: #4507
Engine capacity: 4.5 Liter
Color: Red

The factory completed this car on July 30, 1957, and it was transported to Sweden to run in the 1,000 km Grand Prix on the Kristianstad circuit on August 11, 1957. Maserati was close behind Ferrari in the World Sportscar Championship and needed to win this race for a chance on the title for the last race in Caracas, Venezuela. Furthermore, Maserati wanted to take revenge for the outcome of this race in 1956 that was a disaster for them when none of the factory team cars finished the race. Sweden was an open bill for the company from Modena.

#4507 had a small but significant detail different from the other 450S that was entered in the race (see the #4503 chapter) – it had a small, round single air intake on the nose section and between the engine hood and the right front fender. No other 450S had an air intake in that position. The body of #4507 had the standard large oval radiator intake while the back of the body had four small horizontal oval holes, which helped to clearly distinguish #4507 from its sister car, #4503, which had three holes in the back. All other later 450S had three oval openings in their backs. #4507 was without the headrest that only the customer cars had. Both 450S in Sweden had larger fuel tanks of 184 liters installed instead of 167 liters to be able to cover the 1,000 km with a single refueling.

Ferrari, having won at Buenos Aires and the Mille Miglia, and was second at Nürburgring, fourth at Sebring and fifth at Le Mans, could be almost sure of securing the World Championship if only one of its cars finished among the first five in the Swedish Grand Prix. No new models of note appeared on this occasion. Maserati had entered #4507 and the older #4503 and one 300S whereas Ferrari had four cars: among them two 335S, one for Hill and Collins and the other for Hawthorn and Musso.

The 4.05-mile circuit set amidst heathland and dark, lofty pines was unaltered since 1956, which meant that it was still rather bumpy and narrow here and there, hard on brakes, but highly interesting. From start to finish, this race was dominated by the big 450S. Mike Hawthorn led for six laps, when Moss, who had started in #4503 and later switched to #4507, went past, pitted, and Jean Behra took over. Behra was in great form. Three times he bettered Fangio's lap record, and soon he had shaken off the Ferraris that were already running short of brakes. #4503 was out after transmission trouble. Moss drove all the other

team cars and finished third with the 300S. It was a good day for Maserati, which could catch up in the World Championship.

The Maserati team went back home, and all cars were refreshed. #4507 received a new cylinder head and a new seven-gear selection on an overdrive box with two gears, now fit for the final race of the year.

Late in October, the entire factory team with four cars embarked to the last round of the World Championship, the Grand Prix of Venezuela, held on a street course in Caracas on November 3, 1957, a race that changed the history of Maserati. The factory team's contingent had again both 450S from Sweden, along with a 300S and the 350S with a V12-engine. Englishman Tony Brooks, although under contract with Aston Martin, with Stirling Moss' help, was "loaned" to the Maserati team. In Caracas, both 450S were the fastest cars in practice. Brooks was not unhappy to drive the 450S and could handle the "Bazooka" well. He told one of the authors in 2008, that he liked the gearbox, the chassis was not flexing too much, and he was much impressed by the sheer endless power of the car.

It was a sunny day in Caracas when Moss behind the wheel of #4507 and Behra in #4503, both had a bad start but soon, Behra was leading, while Moss in all his magic, overtook 25 cars in his first lap and was leading the race, cruising at a high speed. Then the American driver, Jo Dressel crossed the path of #4507 in his AC Bristol. Moss could not avoid him and crashed into Dressel, smashing the entire front section of his car. The AC was thrown into the air, hit a lamppost and fell back split in two. Both drivers were lucky to survive this crash without any severe injuries.

It was not a sunny day anymore for #4507 and for the entire Maserati team as all the cars were destroyed later in the race (see the #4503 chapter). The second part of the race turned into a triumphal procession for Ferrari who filled the first four places at the finish and captured the 1957 World Championship title. The situation in Caracas was also a financial disaster for the Modenese company. Maserati race director Nello Ugolini had informed his drivers before the start that all their cars had already been sold after the race with the expected laurels, to wealthy private drivers from South America and therefore every effort should be

The new #4507 in Sweden ready for the technical inspection by the officials of the 1957 Swedish Grand Prix. Maserati pit-lane boss, Guerino Bertocchi, is in the car. *(Klemantaski Collection)*

Moss is ready to try out #4507 during practice session in Sweden in 1957. *(Walter Bäumer Collection)*

OPPOSITE: Behra wins the 1957 Swedish Grand Prix in #4507. The car ran like a clock and dominated the Ferrari opposition *(Walter Bäumer Collection)*

Color photographs from the Grand Prix in Caracas at the end of 1957 are rare. #4507 is lined up in the paddock next to #4503 (no. 2). *(Walter Bäumer Collection)*

OPPOSITE: Moss in the car in Caracas in 1957. Later, the car no longer looked so pretty. *(Walter Bäumer Collection)*

The car after the crash with Jo Dressel's AC Bristol in Caracas.
Moss was lucky to survive the impact. *(Unknown photographer)*

The wreck of #4507 was shipped back to Italy and stored in the factory. The rebuild started in 1959 and the damaged part of the body was cut off, the chassis straightened, and a new suspension fitted. *(Zagari/Spitzley Archive)*

made not to damage them. Each of the 450S had a value of almost US$10,000 – money that was much needed by the factory. After that catastrophic race, all the wrecks were taken back to Italy.

It was always believed that #4507 was the car that ended in flames in Caracas following the impact with the 300S of Bonnier and therefore had later been scrapped by the factory – but this was not the case! The front damage was repaired in the factory and #4507 came out with a shorter nose section. To sell the car would not be easy as after the tragic 1957 Mille Miglia, the FIA changed its rules and permitted only cars from 1958 on with a 3-liter capacity to participate. Another problem was that the Italian government suspended all car and motorcycle races on public roads in Italy following the crash of the Ferrari 335S of de Portago and Nelson in the Mille Miglia in which many spectators died. The partly dismantled #4507 was photographed among the new Tipo 60 Birdcage prototypes in the Maserati factory in March 1959 by legendary US journalist,

Peter Coltrin, who was living in Modena. Two of his photographs clearly show a 450S in the process of rebuilding with freshly welded parts on a new front chassis and showing a half-cut front body waiting for a new skin. The windshield was covered with dust because of a long period of storage and the rear part of the body was still there. Also, there were two small, rounded air intakes on the rear top on each front fender, as on the car in the wreck from Caracas.

The two last 450Ss, completed in January 1958, had already been delivered to the USA one year earlier. This confirms that only one 450S could have been in the factory in March 1959: the surviving 450S from the Caracas disaster. Whether the bodywork was repaired by Fantuzzi is not entirely clear, as he had been working for Ferrari since the end of 1958. The car fitted with a large horizontal air scoop added below the front air opening. Factory documentation indicates that the rebuilt car was sold one year later to Enrique Severino Casini, a rich Brazilian industrialist and motor sport enthusiast, and the owner of Casini

OPPOSITE: #4507 was painted yellow and sold to Brazil. Henrique Casini crashed it in its first outing in an unidentified race. *(FotOld)*

An unknown person kneels beside #4507, now painted red, before the race in Interlagos in September 1961. *(Unknown photographer)*

Rubber Industry in Rio de Janeiro. The 450S was renumbered 345. The car was painted in yellow with two green stripes of 10 cm width, red cloth interior and a black number "6" painted on a white circle, as requested and ordered by Casini. On October 18, 1960, the car was shipped to Brazil from Genoa harbor on the vessel "Augustus". All the details on the bodywork, such as the four oval cuts in the tail helped to identify the 450S in Kristianstad and Caracas as the same 450S seen later in Brazil. Casini was a very good driver and had previously raced a Maserati 300S loaned to Severino Gomez-Silva, #3069, the ex-Fangio winner of the Portugal and Brazil GP in 1957. Casini successfully drove the yellow 300S with race number 6 from March 1958 to May 1959 and won the title of Brazilian Champion in 1958.

#4507 appeared driven by Casini with the national Brazilian colors of yellow with a double green stripe and large stickers "Casini" on both doors. Besides another non-identified race, Casini participated with the 450S in the Grande Premio Cidade do Rio de Janeiro in Barra da Tijuca on November 5, 1960, where, despite having an accident, he finished in fourth place in what was his last race, as he was 62 years old. The magazine *Jornal dos Sport* reported in its November 11, 1960 issue: "...When Henrique Casini had upshifted to minimize his distance to the leading car on lap 21, an imprudent person crossed the track [..] Casini, to avoid being hit by a following car, made a sudden counter steering. His car skidded and hurled itself against a DKW that was unexpectedly parked there, crushing a photographer, who suffered fractures in both legs and slightly hitting two girls and a boy, who refused medical help. Casini was able to continue in the race, but he lost his position and had his nervous system shaken, without the necessary peace of mind to keep racing [...]." The race was won by the Portuguese Mario Cabral with the Maserati 300S of Scuderia Centro Sud.

In end of 1960 Casini sold his 450S to Emílio Zambello. According to the Brazilian source Bandeira Quadriculada, Zambello was born in the city of Padova, Italy and immigrated to Brazil in 1950, aged 23. Then he met another Italian, Ruggero Peruzzo, who worked in a Land Rover workshop and was a good mechanic. They became close friends and bought a workshop in downtown Sao Paulo, which they called "Garage Fulgor." In 1957, also in partnership with Peruzzo, Zambello opened the "Auto Peças Fulgor" store, close to the workshop of Comino, a Weber carburetor maker. Zambello took the damaged 450S from Casini and had it painted red with a double white stripe. As the original engine was then broken, Zambello took a plane to Italy and acquired through Guerino Bertocchi a new Maserati V8 engine numbered 352 which was, as mentioned in the Zagari-Orsini book, invoiced to Brazil on November 12, 1960. First

A great photograph of a relaxed Celso Lara Barberis posing on #4507 at Interlagos. Some details show that the car is far from being in excellent condition. *(Fred J. Maroon Archive/The University of Texas)*

registered race under the Zambello ownership was on January 15, 1961, the Formula Libre "Torneio Sul-Americano" race at Interlagos where Ruggero Peruzzo finished sixth overall in 2 runs of 10 laps.

Moreover, a factory letter signed by Aurelio Bertocchi was sent on February 21, 1983 to Franco Lombardi (see 4501 chapter) referring to Girling upgrades on the 450S-type braking system: "It was on the 450S car no. 345 owned by Signor Zambello of São Paulo in Brazil and this modification, which we personally studied, and was in fact carried out at Maserati with more than satisfactory results."

The car was entered under the Escuderia Tubularte banner for the IV 500 Kilometers of Interlagos on September 7, 1961. Ruggero Peruzzo and Celso Lara Barberis drove, sharing two cars: #4507 with race number 27 which won the race, and a Maserati 300S, loaned by José Gimenez Lopes owner of Tubularte, a kitchen furniture factory, who was ill and could not race. That 300S with race number 28 came in third, only losing second place because of the stops for changing drivers. Emílio Zambello assisted in driving both cars and

was also loaned the 300S of José Gimenez Lopes. The winning 450S had various sponsors, as seen on the front bonnet: "Juntos Dinis" Diniz Seals, and on both sides, "Pirani", one of the main department stores at the time.

A rare period color photograph with a smiling Celso Lara Barberis standing next to the 450S in Interlagos clearly shows the back of the body with the four oval holes. Celso Lara Barberis was an excellent Brazilian driver, having previously raced with the Escuderia Tubularte Maserati 300S at the 1,000 km of Buenos Aires in 1960 finishing fourth co-driving with "Bino" Heinz and winning the III 500 Kilometers of Interlagos in 1960, among other successes with Maserati. In 1962, during the training sessions for the 12 Hours of Interlagos, Zambello met another Italian, Piero Gancia, originally from Turin.

Gancia had established a family company producing vermouth and wines in Brazil. His professional involvement with motor sport began to take shape in Sao Paulo in 1961. After traveling around the city looking for a good mechanic to repair the crankcase of his Alfa Romeo Giulietta TI, he ended up at the Escuderia Tubularte, owned by José Gimenez Lopes. There he met the mechanic and

The big Temple Buell seems much satisfied with his brand new #4508, that Maserati chief mechanic Guerino Bertocchi demonstrated to him on the Aerautodromo in the heart of Modena. On the left is journalist and part-time wheeler dealer Hans Tanner, and in the middle smiling, English Maserati customer Horace Gould. *(Walter Bäumer Collection)*

Masten Gregory gives photographer Tom Burnside a passenger ride from to the pit lane from the workshop in Caracas where Maserati maintained their cars. *(Revs Institute)*

OPPOSITE: Masten Gregory poses next to the new #4508 in the pitlane of the 1957 Venezuelan GP in Caracas. Behind him, with glasses, is Hans Tanner, who acted as team manager for the Temple Buell team, whose principal is the big man behind the pit wall on the right. *(Walter Bäumer Collection)*

Gregory made something wrong and crashed the brand-new car into the sandbags within the first lap, turning it upside down. Mike Hawthorn in his Ferrari 335S passes by. He later finished on second overall position. *(Walter Bäumer Collection)*

OPPOSITE: Masten Gregory survived the crash with only minor injuries thanks to a headrest that had been fitted behind his back in the car just before the race. He had much luck. *(Walter Bäumer Collection)*

and she got away from me, and I hit a fence and rolled over, ending with my wheels in the wall. I managed to kick out before help arrived, but I had broken my goggles and cut myself up a little doing it. Still, who wants to sit upside down under a car?"

Cyril Posthumus wrote in his book *World Sportscar Championship*: "...Gregory's 450S "was flying in the air, having failed to take the turn; it hit the sandbags, bounced, then landed .... On its back..." Incredibly, Gregory crawled out little the worse. What had saved his life was the roll bar under the headrest, on which he had insisted after practice."

During the race, the entire Maserati team cars were involved in crashes, losing the World Championship to Ferrari. Although #4508 looked presentable' when back on its wheels, underneath the damage was more severe. The car was transported to the mechanics, Lee Lilley and Bill Orr, who had their shop called TAMCO in Miami, Florida, for the rebuild. The chassis had some damage, and its body was straightened. Lilley reported later that the car in the accident must have slid upside down on the road, as its Weber carburetors and intake manifolds had to be replaced by parts that were ordered from Italy.

Buell had his repaired car transported to California for the inaugural race on the Riverside circuit on November 16-17, 1957. Again, Masten Gregory, who liked driving powerful, big, heavy cars, was behind the wheel of #4508. He showed the potential of the car, winning race 5 over five laps but in race 10 he was beaten by the winner, Carroll Shelby, in #4506 and Dan Gurney in second in a 4.9-liter Ferrari that had been modified by its owner, Frank Arciero. The next event, the Nassau Speed Week in the Bahamas from December 1-8, 1957, became quite successful for #4508 and Masten Gregory. He won the Tourist

Trophy race and came home third in the sprint race and second in the Governor's Trophy. But in the main race, the Nassau Trophy, Gregory came back to the pits after 13 laps, stepped out of the car, reporting problems with the transaxle. The driveshaft was broken, and the car was shipped back to TAMCO for the repair.

In 1958, Temple Buell hired Carroll Shelby as Masten Gregory had moved to Italy. The "chicken farmer" complained about the uncomfortable position on the seat that had been designed for the smaller Gregory. However, Shelby's #4508 was first over the finish line at Miami, Florida, on January 11-12 for the Orange Bowl race. *Sports Car* wrote: "... [he] won without ever breathing deeply." But Shelby could not finish race 6 due to a broken oil line.

Joel Finn wrote in his book *Caribbean Capers*: "Normally, a broken oil line, if caught in time, is not disastrous. However, in this case, the engine turned out to be seriously wounded, with a damaged crankshaft, burned connecting rods and warped cylinder heads. Mechanics, Lilley and Orr, thought it might be possible to repair the damage in the month remaining before the Cuban race, but Temple Buell decided to take the safe, though expensive, route, and purchase a new engine directly from Maserati. The engine was to be delivered to Havana a week before the race."

The new engine was delayed but finally arrived in New York. It was flown out to Miami but on the first practice day in Cuba. Temple Buell had high hopes for the race and negotiated a deal with Fangio manager Marcello Giambertone for the Cuban GP on February 24, 1958, on the roads of Havana.

Maserati had officially closed its race department and retired from all race activities, and Fangio had also officially retired from racing, it was a good

Back on its 4 wheels on the track after the race in Caracas 1957. The damage to the car does not appear to have been that serious, but this turned out to be wrong a few days later. *(Walter Bäumer Collection)*

OPPOSITE: Two weeks after the crash in Caracas, #4508 was repaired and with Masten Gregory in Riverside. It was a good day for the Temple Buell equipe as Gregory won the race.

(Walter Bäumer Collection)

In Havana in February 1958, surrounded by Cuban Army personal and Police before practice, Juan Manuel Fangio is discussing his drive in #4508. The installation of the new engine had just been completed. *(Walter Bäumer Collection)*

OPPOSITE: Fangio got last advice before taking the car out for practice. The new 4.5-Liter engine reached Havana just in time to be installed in the car and ready for training. *(Unknown photographer)*

After practice, Fangio took General Fernandez Miranda, president of the Sporting Commission in Cuba and so responsible for the race event, into the car for a passenger ride around the course for some laps. A little later, Fidel Castro's boys "invited" the star driver to a ride in one of their cars... *(Klemantaski Collection)*

OPPOSITE: The next day – where is Fangio? All the officials and the policemen seem to be waiting for something that nobody knows what will happen. Maurice Trintignant (with black shirt and googles) is standing at the back of the car, preparing to drive the car in the race. *(Associated Press)*

Carroll Shelby was in #4508 in Riverside in October 1958. His mechanic Joe Landaker mounted the Trident-logo upside down, reflecting his and the driver's mood after practice and the disappointing final result. *(Joel Finn Estate)*

OPPOSITE: Chassis #4508 jacked up beside the truck of John Edgar in Pomona for the Examiner GP. *(Walter Bäumer Collection)*

chance to catch some of the big prize money for the five-times Formula 1 Champion. In addition, Buell paid the organizer, the Sporting Commission in Cuba (CSC) US$5,000 and Fangio another US$5,000. The CSC agreed to pay all expenses to fly Nello Ugolini, Guerino Bertocchi and two Maserati mechanics to Cuba to support the entry of #4508. When the Italians arrived, they quickly noticed that the old engine had a damaged crankshaft. General Fernandez Miranda, president of the CSC and responsible for the entire event was told and he managed to send a Cuban Airforce plane to Miami to collect the new motor. Fangio arrived in Cuba on February 21 and found his car not ready for practice, so he used a privately entered 300S while Guerino Bertocchi and his men installed the new motor.

Race enthusiast, Joel Finn, who was involved in timing for that event by General Electric and IBM, witnessed the engine change and wrote in his book *Caribbean Caper*: "...on arriving at the airport [in Miami, Ed.] it turned out there was only one seat available on that particular flight to Havana. Further, there was no room on the plane to take the Sebring master timing system onboard, which we had brought along with us. I was paged to the Cubana office for a phone call [from the organizer, Ed.]. He told me a Cuban army plane was on its way to the Miami airport to pick up a Maserati engine for Fangio's car that was being held at customs and told me to go to the Intra-Mar shipping office and wait there until it arrived.

"The plane arrived about 8:00pm with Hans Tanner on board, whom I already knew, who had been deputized to get the engine. The customs people would not release the engine to Tanner, who was a Swiss citizen, but only to an American. It didn't matter to the customs people that the engine was immediately going on to Cuba. "Rules is rules" to bureaucrats. So, I signed for the engine and off to Havana we went [...] We landed at Camp Columbia, the government military airfield on the outskirts of the city, about 11:00pm loaded the engine onto an Army truck and about midnight got to the automobile dealership in downtown Havana where the 450S was being worked on.

"Guerino Bertocchi and another Maserati mechanic had already removed the original engine and were ready to install the new unit. However, you don't just drop in a 450S engine. The water pump is jammed tight up against and immediately underneath the front chassis frame tube. To remove the engine, it has to be carefully raised rear-end first at an acute angle. This is after the radiator has been removed, the clutch, driveshaft and exhaust manifolds removed, and the transaxle moved back. The whole process had to be reversed to get the engine installed. With two mechanics working non-stop, the job could be done in eight to ten hours. [...] I headed back to the dealership and slept on an office floor for some time, perhaps an hour. Very loud swearing emanating from the

#4508 was maintained by the John Edgar organization. Here the car is ready to go for Carroll Shelby in California for the Examiner GP in March 1959. Note the taped headlamps to protect them from stone chips. *(Thomas Horat/Motorsportfriends Archive)*

service area soon woke me. It seems the mechanic helping Bertocchi had seriously sliced the webbing of his right hand on a sharp object and was bleeding profusely. After bandaging the wound, it was apparent that he wouldn't be able to do much work the rest of the night. I volunteered to help Bertocchi, if nothing more than to hand him tools or tighten nuts and bolts. He put me to work, and we (mostly he) got the engine installed and running about 07:00am.

"Bertocchi proceeded to drive the 450S up and down the street to check for oil and fuel leaks, carburetor settings and the like. At one point, he put me in the car to work the clutch pedal while he adjusted it. After this little chore was completed, Bertocchi told me to fire up the engine and take the car onto the street to see how everything worked. Words can't describe how thrilled I was, even though my speeds were very modest. Finally, he told me to goose the throttle a few times to ensure the engine would pick up at slow speeds and full throttle. I was only too happy to oblige. The power and force of acceleration were stunning. This started a long-time obsession to someday own that car. Finally, eighteen years later, I was able to get it."

In the practice session on Saturday morning, #4508 was running. Fangio, who had won the race the previous year in a Maserati 300S, was fastest with 1:59:2 min, followed by Moss in a privately-owned Ferrari 335S. Fangio then took General Miranda out for one or two laps for a ride.

On Sunday evening, everybody went back to Hotel Lincoln for relaxation and socializing. There was a strange atmosphere all over the city of Havana as Cuba was on the eve of the Revolution led by Fidel Castro and nobody knew what would happen – and something happened!

Alessandro de Tomaso, who had also traveled to Cuba recounted the events of that night in a report he made to the police. Parts of his narrative were extensively quoted in the Havana newspapers the next day: "Four of us, Fangio, his Maserati team manager Nello Ugolini, Maserati chief mechanic Guerino Bertocchi and me, were standing by the front desk in the hotel Lincoln lobby. We were chatting about the weather and discussing where to have dinner while waiting for Marcello Giambertone to join us. Our tentative plan was to go to some nearby restaurant, have a quick meal and retire early. The hotel lobby was well filled. Groups of drivers here and there, some standing, some sitting, and other guests reading and chatting. I had noticed, but not paid much attention to, three men who would come in the front door, stand there for a few moments, and then go back outside. They didn't seem the least bit threatening in any way. I thought they were Cuban race fans wanting a glimpse of Fangio. It was just about 8.45 PM. when the three men re-entered the hotel lobby. Two remained on either side of the front door while the third, waving what looked like a 45 Colt automatic pistol, strode over quickly to Fangio's chauffeur, who was

Skip Hudson in his Ferrari 410S behind #4508 with Shelby, passing the stranded Lotus 11 of Roy Salvadori at Pomona in March 1959. *(Allen R. Kuhn)*

209

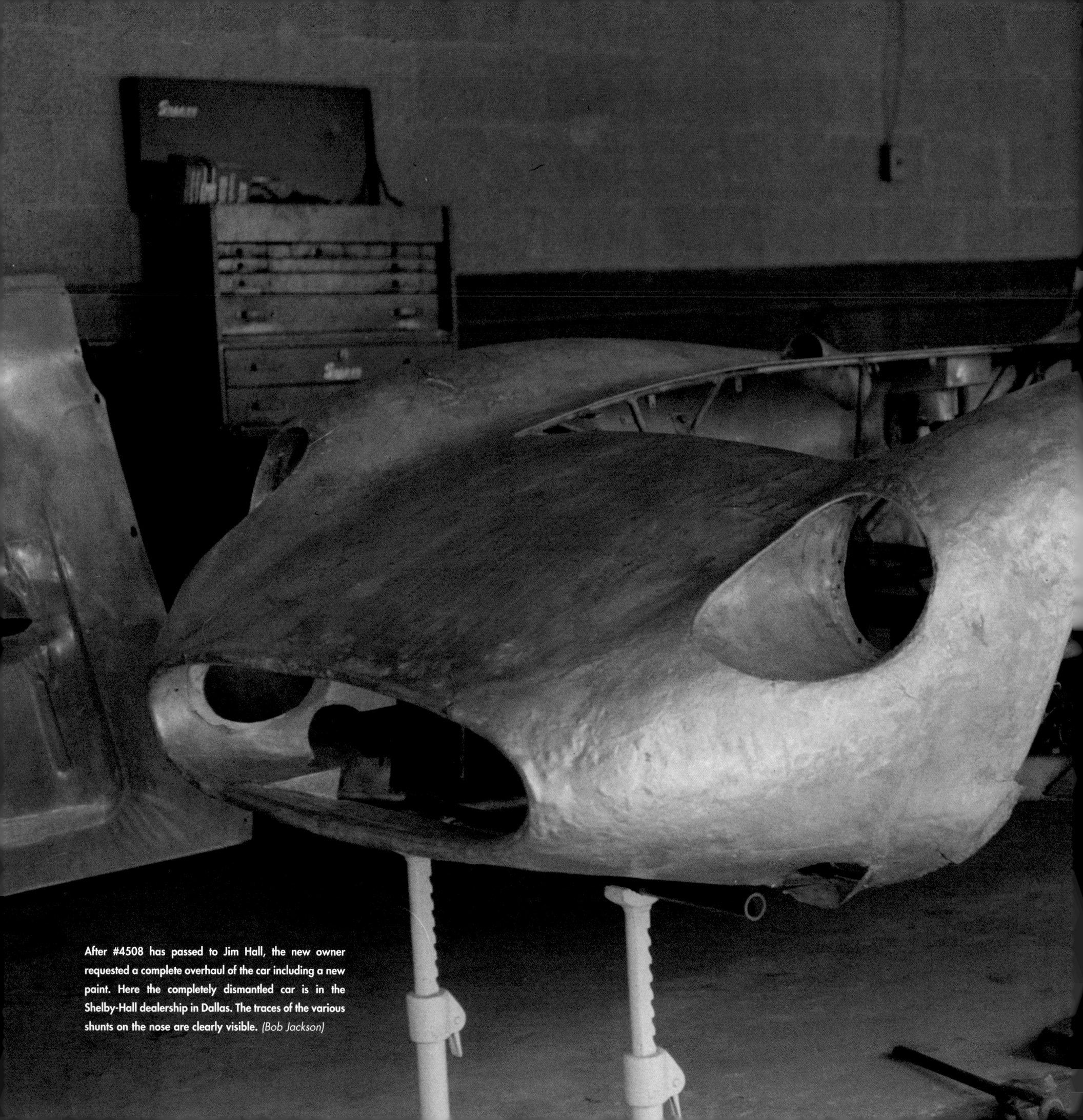

After #4508 has passed to Jim Hall, the new owner requested a complete overhaul of the car including a new paint. Here the completely dismantled car is in the Shelby-Hall dealership in Dallas. The traces of the various shunts on the nose are clearly visible. *(Bob Jackson)*

OPPOSITE: Very few photos are existing that shows Jim Hall smiling. Not even when he was sitting in this now white #4508 that was looking great and in pristine condition after its restoration. *(Bob Jackson)*

Lloyd Ruby jacked up in the rear in the pits of Nassau in December 1959, where he had taken over the car from Carroll Shelby. *(FORD Museum/T.Friedman)*

standing by himself a few feet from us and frisked him. At the same moment, the other two strangers pulled out pistols and covered the room. Everything instantly became deathly quiet in the lobby, and everybody froze in position. Satisfied that the chauffeur was unarmed, the man then approached us and said, "Which one of you is Fangio?" "I am," Fangio answered. "What do you want?"

"I want you to come with me. I'm from the 26th of July Movement. Don't resist and you won't be hurt!" Once more the man warned: "Don't move or I'll shoot." His voice, his manner, everything about him showed utter calm and determination. Nobody moved. They disappeared out the door. The other two gunmen waited a few more seconds before they too backed out the door while continuing to cover us with their pistols. The whole kidnapping operation couldn't have taken much more than a minute. We heard several cars driving away in opposite directions, but there were no screeching tires or loud engine noises. It was all very deliberate and designed not to draw attention to themselves. We waited a while, maybe 30 or 45 seconds, and then ran out. They were gone, vanished into the night.

"We had the desk clerk call to notify the police about the kidnapping. At first, the police didn't believe the clerk, thinking it must be some kind of hoax or publicity stunt. I then called Giambertone's room and told him what had happened. Giambertone immediately phoned Ernesto Azua Font, the director of the Grand Prix to report the news to him. Within ten minutes, the hotel lobby was crammed with police and army personnel, all wanting to know what had happened and seeking clues as to who the kidnappers were and where they had gone. We couldn't help them in any way. The police also posted heavily armed guards all around the hotel in case the Communists might try to snatch other important drivers. In our minds, the ones that were at greatest risk were Stirling Moss and Jim Kimberly, the latter as he was a very wealthy capitalist, a type of person anathema to the Communists.

"We turned on the radio and televisions in the lobby at about 8.55 PM only ten minutes after the abduction, to find that the Communists had already notified all the media. The revolutionaries accused the Cuban government of promoting a "Roman Spectacle" while 500,000 Cubans had no jobs."

Giambertone and de Tomaso drove to the local radio station for a speech to convince Castro's boys to release the Argentinian race star, while the police and heavily-armed Cuban soldiers were flooding the city, searching for him. Since Fangio's whereabouts had still not been clarified and a speedy release was not to be expected, Buell gave the 450S to French driver Maurice Trintignant, who had never driven one of these big V8s before. On race day, #4508 was then pushed to Trintignant's pole position in the fifth row he had achieved during practice in a Jaguar D-Type. His race in #4508 was not spectacular and he finished eleventh overall.

After a lot of diplomatic and private efforts, Fangio was released on the afternoon of the race day, with a "Please excuse us for having inconvenienced you" and returned to the Argentine Embassy. But being the star driver, he received his US$5,000 start money from the organizers. The kidnapping caused a lot of attention and media coverage all over the world.

Back in the US, #4508 was shipped to La Junta in Colorado for the race on May 31 to June 1, 1958, for Temple Buell's buddy Dabney Collins, but he could not finish the race due to a loss of oil pressure. It is not clear which engine was installed in the car. Some sources mentioned that it was an experimental 5- or 5.1-liter unit and that the car had been sent to the factory in Italy for a technical upgrade, but records from the factory archive state that it was returned two months later, in July. Book author Willem Oosthoek believes that it was still the 4.7-liter version that was installed in the car in Cuba.

Carroll Shelby was back in #4508 on October 12, 1958, for the Times Grand Prix in Riverside. The car showed some wear on its front section, and mechanic Joe Landaker had put the famous Trident logo upside down in the radiator opening. Shelby was completely disappointed by the performance and retired the car on its fourth lap with a blown head gasket. But interestingly, Shelby in his biography Shelby, the Race Driver by Art Evans reported that the reason for the retirement was "…two of the cylinders in the Maserati quit".

Stirling Moss was supposed to drive #4508 in the race, but he canceled due to problems with the organizers as reported in a letter Moss wrote to MotoRacing that was published on November 7, 1958.

The next venue for #4508 was in Palm Springs, California, on November 2, 1958, again with Shelby as its driver. Interestingly, the press noted a 5.7-liter engine that was numbered #4511. It seems that this engine had been installed in Italy, at some point after the race at La Junta. Shelby won the race with a 22-second lead ahead of Max Balchowsky in his 5.2-liter Old Yeller.

Back to the Nassau Speed Week in the Bahamas, #4508 looked battered. Shelby did not start in the Governor's Trophy, saving the car for the main race, the Nassau Trophy on December 7, 1958. During that race, one of the rear tires damaged a battery terminal, and when Shelby pitted he could not restart to return into the race.

At the Pomona meet from March 7-8, 1959, there was a race that saw four 450S on the grid: Shelby again in #4508, now entered by John Edgar, Ebb Rose in #4509, Hal Ullrich with #4504 and Bill Krause in #4502 who finally was the happy winner in race 6, with Carroll Shelby only eleventh. In race 11, the Los Angeles Examiner GP, #4508 did not see the finish.

Temple Buell Jr. then lost interest in motor sport and moved his 450S to Dallas where it was stored for several months in the Carroll Shelby and Dick Hall dealership. A young Jim Hall wanted to drive it in Stuttgart, Arkansas, for the Inaugural Sports car races on April 18-19, 1959, but a mechanic damaged its transmission, and the car could not be used in that race.

OPPOSITE: The white #4508 under maintenance by chief mechanic Red Byron for the event in Palm Springs in January 1960. *(Bob Jackson)*

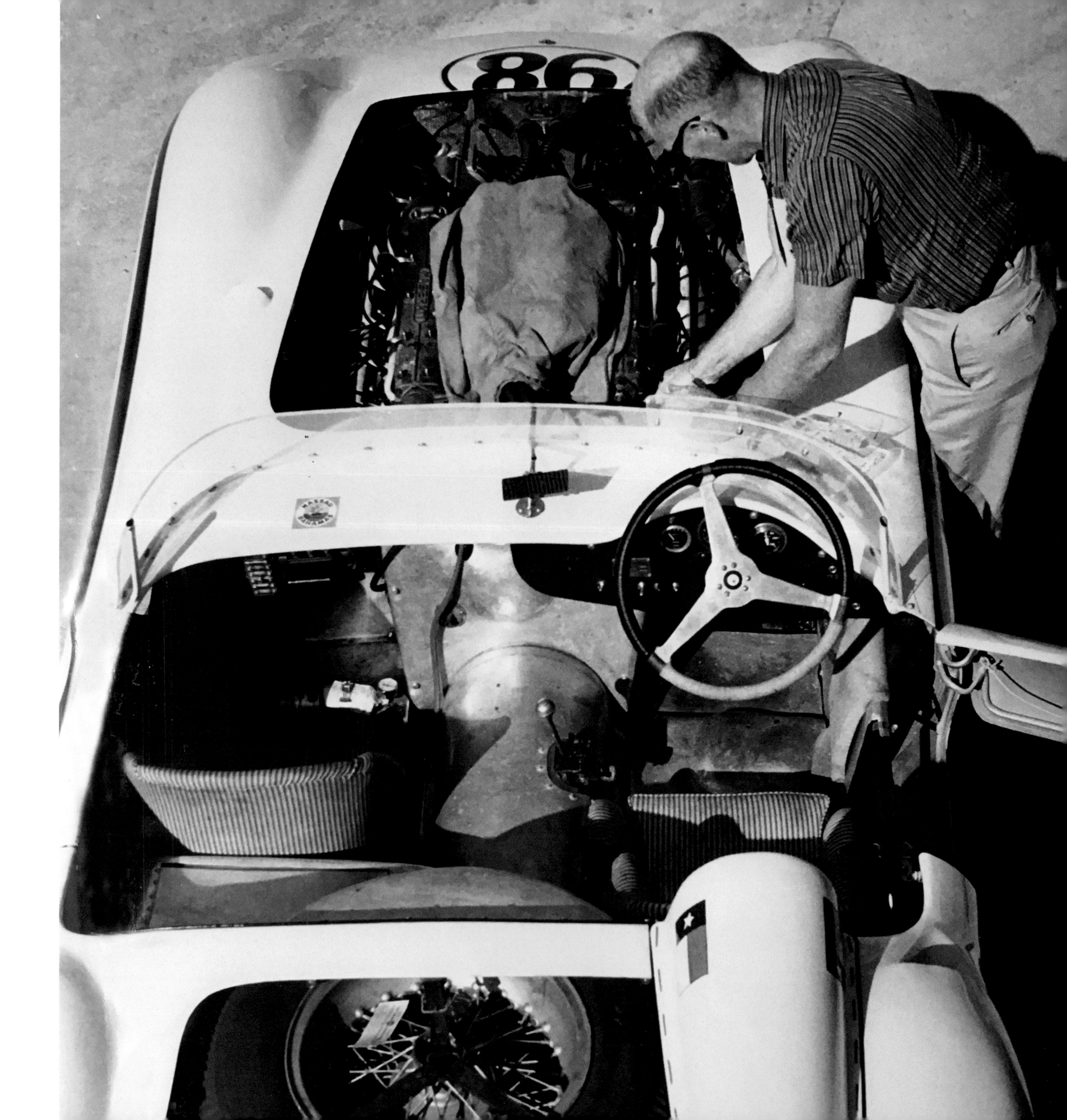

The 450S of Jim Hall in Mansfield on the DeSoto Parish Airport in March 1961. The rear Borrani wire wheels had been removed and replaced by Halibrands with new steel hubs. The now aging car still showed it muscle's and saw the checkered flag as the winner. *(Bob Jackson)*

Jim Hall pushes his white monster to the grid for the race in Mansfield with mechanics Frank Lance (left)and Billy Billings. *(Bob Jackson)*

#4508 was offered for sale by the Carroll Shelby-Dick Hall dealership in *Sports Car*, the magazine of the Sports Car Club of America (SCCA) in the August 1959 issue with an asking price of US$8,500.

Jim Hall made an offer for the blue/white powerhouse and owner Buell accepted. However, Hall was not satisfied with the worn-out condition of #4508 and decided on an overhaul and the car was completely dismantled under the supervision of chief mechanic, Robert "Red" Byron, who had worked previously for Briggs Cunningham and Corvette. The Jim Hall crew – Byron, Frank Lance, Foy Barrett and Bob Schroeder worked from September to November 1959 at the Yale Boulevard workshop in Dallas. The 5.7- liter V8 engine was rebalanced by Bob Johnson of Dallas. The car had a bigger, less elegant bulk now on its front bonnet, covering the longer Weber pipes. The steering wheel was refitted at a much-inclined angle to accommodate Shelby and Hall who were both tall. For the Nassau Speed Week from December 31 to December 6, 1959, the refreshed car, now with Shelby's race number 98, was back in bright white paint with a long waved, thin blue stripe on each side. The seats were upholstered to match Carroll Shelby's striped bib overalls.

Three of the new, much lighter Maserati Tipo 61 "Birdcages" had been shipped by their owners to the Bahamas, clearly introducing a more modern chapter in motor sport. Carroll Shelby drove the car to third place in the sprint race over 5 laps. In the Governor's Trophy over 12 laps, Shelby could not finish as #4508 had brake problems. The next day, in the main race, the Nassau Trophy over 55 laps, Shelby drove one of the new Birdcages but pulled out due to transmission trouble. Lloyd Ruby started in his own 450S (see the #4509 chapter) but had engine problems and after the first lap returned to the pits. He jumped out of his car and into #4508 to continue in the race but finished fifteenth.

The first event for the white #4508 in 1960 was in the Palm Springs races on January 23-24. Jim Hall had his first competition in his car in race 7 over 5 laps and finished fourth overall but had bad luck the next day in race 14 when he could not finish. Six weeks later, Hall was in Mansfield, Louisiana and finished third in race 4 over 8 laps but was out in the first lap in race 7 when the plugs failed. Then back to California on April 3, 1960, Jim Hall was on the very hot Riverside Raceway for the Examiner GP and he was the seventh fastest in the Consolation race. In the main race, the #4508's transmission broke and Hall could only watch the race as a spectator.

In June 1961, Lloyd Ruby was behind the wheel of #4508 in the Hoosier GP at Indianapolis. In race 1 he reached the finish line as the winner and in race 2 he came home as second. Here he is leading Ken Miles in his Porsche. *(Walter Bäumer Collection)*

The Carrera del Alamo races in San Marcos, Texas, followed on April 17, 1960. Jim Hall drove for three hours from Dallas to the circuit with his Maserati 3500GT with one-off Allemano coachwork. In the race, he had a bad start in #4508 but finished in third place in race 5 over 10 laps but in race 8, he was leading the race, although chased by the new Maserati Birdcage of oilman Jack Hinkle and saw the finish line as the winner! Hall showed the 10,000 spectators that the "truck" could still be very fast with a great performance. On May 1, 1960, Hall tried the modern Maserati Birdcage he had purchased from Lucky Casner and won with it at Longview, Texas. On July 3, he had both Maseratis at Galveston, Texas and drove both cars in practice but finally decided on the big V8 because it was the faster car. It was the right decision as he won both the sprint race with 10 laps and race 6 with 20 laps. The big white banger was back! Continental Divide Raceway in Colorado saw the same successful result, but in race 7 Hall left the road with a damaged front tire. He pitted, replaced the tires, drove back on the track but had to give up in lap 23 when the car had transmission problems. Together with his Birdcage, the 450S was refurbished in Hall's shop at Greenville Avenue, Dallas and received a small windshield for the driver and a tonneau over the co-driver's seat.

The Times GP at Riverside on October 16, 1960, saw no less than nine of the very competitive Maserati Birdcages and many other strong cars. Hall was seventh fastest in qualifying but saw the checkered flag in ninth place after 62 laps.

But the writing was on the wall for the Maserati 450S as it was losing its competitiveness to much smaller, lighter cars with better chassis and brakes. Hall told the US magazine *Road & Track*: ""I guess I've thought about selling or retiring the 5.7-liter car many times. It is a brute to drive, and it leaves you tired after working it around. But that Maserati almost has a personality. It's got quite a background in competition. The car has so much fire and go, and it really sounds like a racing machine. I like to drive it for those reasons alone. Of course, it won't handle like a Birdcage, few cars do, but whenever you want to go, plenty of it, that Maser's got it." His last race in his 450S was at Mansfield, Louisiana, on March 11, 1961. After 20 laps, #4508 bid him farewell as the winner of the race.

Hall sold #4508 to the car enthusiast Frank Harrison from Chattanooga, Tennessee, whose family owned the Chattanooga Glass Company and was connected with the Coca-Cola empire. Harrison had seen Fangio and Behra win at Sebring in 1957 and was much impressed by the looks and performance of this Maserati. #4508 became the third 450S in his stable (see the #4509 and #4510 chapters).

He engaged Lloyd Ruby to drive the car at Hoosier GP on the Indianapolis Raceway Park, Indiana on June 25, 1961, now with its race number 1. Ruby was the fourth fastest in qualifying but gunned the car in heat 1 after 40 laps to the finish line as the winner, beating the Porsche RS61 of Ken Miles and Augie Pabst in the strong 5.6-liter Scarab. Although Ruby's driving style was spectacular, it was Pabst in first place in heat 2 over Ruby in second. On its second race in Harrison's ownership at Courtland, Alabama on July 2, 1961, the white 450S was in the hands of Bill Kimberly but only went 20 yards before the differential broke.

Chassis #4508 with its current owner but back in the 1980s in Elkhart Lake.
(Walter Bäumer Collection)

After that race in Courtland, the car was retired and stored by Frank Harrison and finally went to Graham Shaw in Columbia, South Carolina, who then sold it to Jack McCann of Huntington Beach, California. Breene Kerr, from Oklahoma City, became the car's owner in 1970. He commissioned a restoration at the Alf Francis shop in Oklahoma. In the early 1950s, Francis had been Stirling Moss's mechanic. Kerr displayed the car in his museum for about eight years until he sold it at auction to collector Peter Livanos, from Connecticut. One year later, it was back on the West Coast, now owned by Howard Cohen from Tiburon, California. A dealer and racer from New York acquired the car in 1983 and drove it in many historic races in the USA. In 2023, he still has it in his possession.

4508 RACE HISTORY

03	Nov.	1957	Venezuela GP, Caracas	Masten Gregory/Dale Duncan (no. 10) DNF, crash
16	Nov.	1957	Riverside, California, race 5	Masten Gregory (no. 4) 1.OA
01	Dec.	1957	Tourist Trophy, Nassau, Bahamas	Masten Gregory (no. 4) 1.OA
06	Dec.	1957	Governor's Trophy, Nassau, Bahamas, heat B, C & D	Masten Gregory (no. 4) 2.OA – 2.i.C.
06	Dec.	1957	Nassau Trophy, Nassau, Bahamas	Masten Gregory (no. 4) DNF
08	Dec.	1957	Governor's Trophy, Nassau, Bahamas	Masten Gregory (no. 4) 2.OA
11	Jan.	1958	Miami, Florida, Orange Bowl, race 1	Carroll Shelby (no. 98) 1.OA
12	Jan.	1958	Miami, Florida, Orange Bowl, race 6	Carroll Shelby (no. 98) DNF
24	Feb.	1958	Cuba GP, Havana	Maurice Trintignant (no. 2) 11.OA
31	May	1958	La Junta, Colorado, race 2	Dabney Collins (no. 24) DNF
12	Oct.	1958	Times GP, Riverside, California	Carroll Shelby (no. 78) DNF
02	Nov.	1958	Palm Springs, California, Exhibition race	Carroll Shelby (no. 78) 1.OA
05	Dec.	1958	Governor's Trophy, Nassau, Bahamas	Carroll Shelby (no. 98) DNS
07	Dec.	1958	Nassau Trophy, Nassau, Bahamas	Carroll Shelby (no. 98) DNF
07	March	1959	Pomona, California, race 6	Carroll Shelby (no. 98) 11.OA
08	March	1959	Los Angeles Examiner GP, Pomona, California	Carroll Shelby (no. 98) DNF
18-19	April	1959	Stuttgart, Arkansas	Jim Hall (no. 98) DNS
04	Dec.	1959	Governor's Trophy, Nassau, Bahamas	Carroll Shelby (no. 98) 3.OA – 1.i.C
04	Dec.	1959	Nassau Trophy, Nassau, Bahamas	Lloyd Ruby (no. 98) 15.OA
23	Jan.	1960	Palm Springs, California, race 7	Jim Hall (no. 98) 4.OA
24	Jan.	1960	Palm Springs, California, race 14	Jim Hall (no. 98) DNF
06	March	1960	Mansfield, Louisiana, race 4	Jim Hall (no. 66) 3.OA
06	March	1960	Mansfield, Louisiana, race 7	Jim Hall (no. 66) DNF
03	April	1960	Consolation race, Riverside, California	Jim Hall (no. 66) 7.OA
03	April	1960	Examiner GP, Riverside, California	Jim Hall (no. 66) DNF
17	April	1960	Carrera del Alamo, San Marcos, Texas, race 5	Jim Hall (no. 66) 3.OA
17	April	1960	Carrera del Alamo, San Marcos, Texas, race 8	Jim Hall (no. 66) 1.OA
03	July	1960	Galveston, Texas, race 3	Jim Hall (no. 66) 1.OA
03	July	1960	Galveston, Texas, race 6	Jim Hall (no. 66) 1.OA
16	July	1960	Continental Divide Raceways, Colorado, race 4	Jim Hall (no. 66) 1.OA
17	July	1960	Continental Divide Raceways, Colorado, race 7	Jim Hall (no. 66) DNF
16	Oct.	1960	Times GP, Riverside, California	Jim Hall (no. 166) 9.OA
11	March	1961	Mansfield, Louisiana	Jim Hall (no. 66) 1.OA
25	June	1961	Hoosier GP/Indianapolis, Indiana, race 1	Lloyd Ruby (no. 1) 1.OA
25	June	1961	Hoosier GP/Indianapolis, Indiana, race 2	Lloyd Ruby (no. 1) 2.OA
02	July	1961	Courtland, Alabama, race 2	Bill Kimberly (no. 1) DNF

4509

Completed: January 28, 1958
Engine #4509
Capacity: 4.5 Liter
Color: Red

Jess E. "Ebb" Rose of Houston, Texas, ran a transportation company in the 1950s and was an enthusiastic racer, having started his career with small Midgets and stockcars and then Corvettes. Next, he purchased the ex-Cunningham 300S, #3052, and later ordered a new 300S, #3073, via Maserati Corporation of America (MCA), the official Maserati importer for the USA in New York. Rose saw the brutish performance of the big V8s from Modena and wanted one of these monsters. As MCA was closed when Maserati retired from all race activities, he ordered a new 450S from the factory via the Dallas Maserati dealership that was run by Dick and Jim Hall and Carroll Shelby.

The car, #4509, was completed on January 28, 1958, and had no holes for brake cooling. It is unknown when the car was finally shipped to the USA. Historians Willem Oosthoek and Michel Bollée wrote in their book about the 450Ss: "… [Shelby and Hall dealership] employee Bob Schroeder remembered the title transfer [of #4509] in a coffee shop at Love Field near Dallas a week before Galveston. Rose flew in to complete the paperwork and settle the bill. He paid cash for his latest fleet addition and while the documents were sorted out, laid his Colt 45 atop a stack of bills totaling US$12,000. The responsibility of depositing the money at Republic Bank the next day was given to Hall rather than Shelby."

#4509 was transported to Galveston, Texas, for the 2nd Gran Carrera Lafitte races, held at Scholes Field, the Galveston municipal airport on April 19-20, 1958. Carroll Shelby himself delivered the new car to its owner. He tested #4509 for Rose over some laps to check if everything was working, followed by Ebb Rose driving his 300S. He watched how Shelby braked and brought the big car into corners. Shelby was very busy that weekend as he also tested Rose's 300S #3073 and a Maserati 250S.

Ebb Rose was a good driver and quickly learned to handle his big Maserati. He finished in first overall place with #4509 in both races that weekend.

The car was in Ft. Worth, Texas, for the races held on the Eagle Mountain National Guard Base from June 7-8,1958. Rose was there with his 300S and the 450S but drove the smaller car in the race after #4509 had some engine problems during practice. Rose then sent the car back to the factory in Italy for a complete engine overhaul. Now in great tune, the car was back in the USA and appeared again in Ft. Worth for the 1st Fall Roundup sports car races at Eagle Mountain on October 11-12, 1958.

Ebb Rose practiced with both his 300S and #4509 but finally chose the 450S for the races. A good choice as the fresh engine in the car placed him first overall in both races 3 and 6.

On November 30, 1958, the 450S was in Hammond, Louisiana. In the meantime, since the Ft. Worth races, Micro-Lube, a Dallas-based manufacturer of fuel and oil additives, had offered Rose sponsorship money. At Hammond, #4509 appeared in the new sponsorship colors, dark blue with a big white stripe. Micro-Lube became the sponsor of all three Maserati that were owned by Ebb Rose which were all renamed "Micro-Lube Specials," written on both sides of each car. #4509 was again the winning car in Hammond, making its owner and sponsor happy.

The new season for the car started on March 7 and 8, 1959 in the Examiner GP in Pomona, California. But the car did not see the checkered flag in race 6 on that day and was not among the starters for race 11 the next day.

Lloyd Ruby, Ebb Rose's mechanic and his driver for all Maserati, was behind the wheel of #4509 on the International Speedway in Daytona, Florida for the 1,000 km race on April 5, 1959, but it was not a good day for the car or for the other cars in that race (see the #4502 and #4506 chapters). Ruby returned to the pits, soaked in oil and with a severe cramp in his leg. Bill Krause, out with #4502, took over #4509 and also came back. He recalled many years later: "…I only did a short stint in the Rose 4.5. That car was dumping oil into the cockpit while going through the banking. The slushing oil in the cockpit got on the left rear tire, which put me in the sand at one time. I was called in, Shelby [who had retired the Rose-owned 300S with a 6.3-Chevy engine] took over, and he soon retired the car. " The cause for this retirement after a total of 110 laps was a broken oil line that could not be fixed.

Ebb Rose became the first owner of #4509. He had ordered the car via the dealership of Carroll Shelby and paid in cash. *(Walter Bäumer Collection)*

OPPOSITE: Ebb had his first successful ride in his new acquisition in Galveston in April 1958. It had the big bulge of the later cars on its hood, covering the carburetors. *(Jean-François Blachette Collection)*

#4509 appeared in the colors of sponsor Micro-Lube. Here Ebb Rose's driver Lloyd Ruby poses together with an unknown beauty next to the car in Daytona in April 1959. *(Unknown photographer)*

OPPOSITE: The car was pushed in the paddock of Daytona for the race over 1,000 km where it was driven by Lloyd Ruby, Bill Krause, and Carroll Shelby in April 1959. Unfortunately, the car did not finish the race. *(FORD Museum/Dave Friedman)*

A great shot of Ruby driving #4509 through the banking at Daytona. The car was also driven by Carroll Shelby, and Bill Krause had a very short stint in it. But in the end, the car was a non-finisher. *(FORD Museum/Dave Friedman)*

An atmospheric photograph of Ruby in #4509 during the Kiwanis GP in Riverside. *(FORD Museum/Dave Friedman)*

OPPOSITE: A posse of Porsches, driven by Bob Holbert (11), Sam Weiss (55) Ken Miles (50) and Ricardo Rodriguez chased the big iron of Lloyd Ruby at Riverside in July 1959. All cars finished the race. *(Allen R. Kuhn)*

On May 31,1959, the big Scarab with the 5.5-liter engine, driven by Jim Jeffords, was the winner in the race at Meadowdale in Illinois, beating Lloyd Ruby in #4509 in second place. During the race, the car touched a wall. Ruby had to go to the pits to check how serious the damage was but was able to return to the track.

#4509 with Ruby was one of the few cars that made it to Lime Rock in Connecticut on June 6, 1959. Ruby was the fastest in practice and started the race in pole position. He was dancing with the car and gunned it with verve around the course, but on lap 44, a tire burst, and he came back to the pits. Changing the wheel cost him four laps and when he had fought back to fifth place, the race was stopped due to heavy rain.

Back at Meadowdale on July 5, Ruby in #4509 was again beaten by the fast Scarab of Jim Jeffords, but he made it to third overall on the podium behind Augie Pabst in his Ferrari.

The next venue for Ruby and #4509 was the Kiwanis GP at Riverside on July 19, 1959, against strong opposition. It is unknown why Ruby could not fully compete with his big Maserati. He was beaten by a smaller Porsche RSK, a Ferrari TR, and the winning Ferrari 412MI of Richie Ginther, finishing in a disappointing ninth place.

On September 5-6, 1959, Ruby had revenge on Jeffords in a Formula Libre race at Meadowdale and sent the Scarab to second place in race 3 but was second in heats 1 and 2 behind Augie Pabst in another Scarab.

Another finish as second overall came at Riverside for the Times GP on October 11, 1959. He was timed as fastest with 157.89 mph in practice. Just after the start, Ruby was behind Chuck Daigh in #4506. Then the race was stopped due to an accident between two Ferraris. After the restart, and after 62 laps, Ruby crossed the finish line behind Phil Hill in his Ferrari 250TR.

Ruby had a bad start in #4509 in Nassau International Trophy on December 6, the last race for the car in 1959, almost immediately losing its rear end and stopping at the pits. Since Carroll Shelby had chosen a Tipo 61 Birdcage for the race, Jim Hall's #4508 sat around unused. After the leaders passed on their second lap, Ruby jumped into that car and finished with it in fifteenth place.

Ruby had a bad start with the big V8 in Nassau, early in December 1959. *(FORD Museum/Dave Friedman)*

Lloyd Ruby's last drive with Ebb Rose's 450S was at Riverside for the Examiner GP in April 1960. *(Walter Bäumer Collection)*

Old against new, Ruby chased Carroll Shelby in a Tipo 61 Birdcage, a car that became one of the driving forces in American sports car racing. Shelby was one lap ahead but the brutish power of the 450S put Ruby into the same lap but not for long. *(Walter Bäumer Collection)*

OPPOSITE: A fantastic photograph of Ruby throwing #4509 through a corner at Riverside. He was one of the drivers who could handle the big car well. *(Walter Bäumer Collection)*

After Frank Harrison became the new owner of #4509 in 1960, the car changed hands again in 1963 to Wick Williams who kept the car dark in its blue color but took away the white stripe. He drove it in only two races in Courtland. Due to heating problems, a rectangular opening had been cut in the nose just over the radiator opening, covered by an adjustable flap. It was a crude modification. *(Unknown photographer)*

Young Wick Williams had style. His helmet was
the same color as his #4508. *(Brannon Collection)*

On April 3, 1960, Lloyd Ruby was seated in #4509 at Riverside for the Examiner GP. Carroll Shelby was driving in a Tipo 61 Birdcage and was leading the race one lap ahead of Ruby but shortly after he unlapped himself, the big V8 was out due to engine problems.

During the practice for the Road America 200 miles in Wisconsin on July 31, 1960, #4509's engine caused trouble again and Ruby was forced to retire. It was Lloyd Ruby's last ride in the blue and white 450S. In September 1960, Ebb Rose had an offer from Frank Harrison from Chattanooga, Tennessee for the car that he accepted. The new owner of the car never entered it for another race. Over time, Harrison owned three of these big Maseratis (see the #4508 and #4510 chapter).

The car was stored for some years and then sold in 1963 via Harrison's mechanic Jerry Eisert to Wick Williams, a student and member of the Sherwin-Williams paint empire from Cleveland. He kept the car in blue but without is white stripe and cut a square opening covered by a flap in its upper front to improve engine cooling. The large squared rear-view mirror as seen with Lloyd Ruby's last races was still there. Wick Williams drove the car on June 8, 1963, in the preliminary race in Courtland but could not finish as the fuel pipe broke in his last lap. Almost one month later, Williams finished ninth, again at Courtland. He offered the car for sale in *Competition Press* in June 1964, asking US $3,900.

Around 1969, the car was in the Larz Anderson Auto Museum. Car hunter Colin Crabbe recalled later: "... In 1971, I had been tipped off that the Larz Anderson Auto Museum in Brookline, Massachusetts, had received a donation of a 1957 Maserati 450S (#4509) and a 1956 Ferrari 410 Sport (#0596), both models thought to have been the most powerful sports racing cars of the 1950s. The Ferrari had been bought originally by the Swede Sture Nottorp for Masten Gregory to drive at the 1957 Nassau Speed Week and the Maserati was the other 450S imported by Shelby in 1958. I was fortunate in being able to buy both cars with the help of Ed Roy, a charming American and the best model maker ever. [...] The cars were brought back to England thinking, perhaps rashly, to sell the Ferrari and keep the Maserati for me to compete with." Crabbe had paid US$5,000 for #4509.

In 1971, the new owner of #4509 became John Fellowes who was from Slough and a member of the British Parliament, who entrusted the car to Trevor Stokes for restoration. The original motor was missing but Stokes was able to find it and put it back in the car. It was also converted to disc brakes, with the rear coming from a Tipo 61. The car was road registered YFL 714H.

In this guise, journalist Alan Henry wrote a feature about the car for Motor Sport in its October and November 1974 issues.

Fellowes sold #4509 in 1979 to collector and amateur racer Bob Sutherland from Colorado, USA. He kept the car for seven years until he sold it to Japan, where it became part of the great collection of Yoshiyuki Hayashi. In 1995, it was back in the UK, now in the hands of noted collector Harry Leventis who had bought it via the UK dealer Talacrest Ltd.

Peter Groh, a dealer from Gärtringen in Germany purchased it in the same year and offered it to respected dealer Klaus Werner from Wuppertal, Germany. He had the car on display at his stand at the Techno Classica car show in Essen, Germany, in April 1996.

US broker Keith Duly managed a deal, and the car crossed the Atlantic to be owned by Myron Schuster in New York. He commissioned a restoration in the shop of Manny Dragone in Connecticut. It changed hands again in 2002, and was owned by Scott Rosen, who was also from New York. He sent the car to Frank Triarsi for another restoration that was incorrect in some details. Rosen sold the car to Marvin Schein, also from New York and sold it a little later to Oscar Davis who kept it in his collection until his passing. His estate gave the car to RM Sotheby's who could not sell it in their auction in Monterey in August 2022, but the car was sold post-auction to a dealer in Canada who had plans to restore it but little later sold it on to a collector in Germany.

BOTTOM AND OPPOSITE: Chassis #4509 in two races in Silverstone when owned In the UK during the 1970s. *(Walter Bäumer Collection)*

4509 RACE HISTORY

20	April	1958	2nd Gran Carrera Lafitte races, Galveston, Texas, race 4	Ebb Rose (no. 45) 1.OA
20	April	1958	2nd Gran Carrera Lafitte races, Galveston, Texas, race 7	Ebb Rose (no. 45) 1.OA
08	June	1958	Ft. Worth, Texas	Ebb Rose (no. 45) DNS
12	Oct.	1958	1st Fall Roundup, Ft. Worth, Texas, race 3	Ebb Rose (no. 45) 1.OA
12	Oct.	1958	1st Fall Roundup, Ft. Worth, Texas, race 6	Ebb Rose (no. 45) 1.OA
30	Nov.	1958	Hammond, Louisiana, race 6	Ebb Rose (no. 45) 1.OA
07	March	1959	Examiner GP, Pomona, California, race 6	Ebb Rose (no. 245) DNF
08	March	1959	Examiner GP, Pomona, California, race 11	Ebb Rose (no. 245) DNS
05	April	1959	1,000 km Daytona, Florida	Lloyd Ruby/Bill Krause/Carroll Shelby (no. 45) DNF
31	May	1959	Meadowdale, Illinois	Lloyd Ruby (no. 45) 2.OA
06	June	1959	Lime Rock, Connecticut	Lloyd Ruby (no. 45) 5.A
05	July	1959	Meadowdale, Illinois	Lloyd Ruby (no. 45) 3.OA
19	July	1959	Kiwanis GP, Riverside, California	Lloyd Ruby (no. 45) 9.OA
06	Sept.	1959	Meadowdale, Illinois, race 3	Lloyd Ruby (no. 45) 1.OA
06	Sept.	1959	Meadowdale, Illinois, main	Lloyd Ruby (no. 45) 2.OA
11	Oct.	1959	Times GP, Riverside, California	Lloyd Ruby (no. 45) 2.OA
06	Dec.	1959	Nassau Trophy, Nassau, Bahamas	Lloyd Ruby (no. 51) DNF
03	April	1960	Examiner GP, Riverside, California	Lloyd Ruby (no. 45) DNF
31	July	1960	Road America 200, Wisconsin	Lloyd Ruby (no. 45) DNS
08-09	June	1963	Courtland, Alabama	Wick Williams (no. 22) DNF, fuel line on last lap
06	July	1963	Courtland, Alabama	Wick Williams (no. 22) 9.OA

4510

Completed: January 28, 1958
Engine: #4510
Engine capacity: 4.5 Liter
Color: Red

This car was the last 450S of the series. It was ordered by Carroll Shelby and Dick Hall's dealership at 5611 Yale Boulevard in Dallas, Texas, for J. Frank Harrison from Chattanooga, Tennessee. Harrison, a wealthy industrialist closely connected with Coca-Cola, was a racing enthusiast and much impressed with the look and brutish performance of the car.

Unfortunately, the exact order date for this car is not recorded in the factory archive but it was shipped to Dallas via sea freight on February 3 and arrived there on March 31, 1958. Harrison had paid US$16,180 for the car, which was enormous money in those days. The car came without holes for brake cooling and had a bigger bulge on its front bonnet to cover the carburetor pipes. Harrison was not a race driver and gave the car to some of his friends to drive. The first race event for the fresh car was at Chester, South Carolina on May 16, 1958, with VW dealer, Dan Clippenger. Although he spun in it in its maiden race, #4510 finished successfully as first overall. Clippinger was again behind the wheel of the car at Ft. Worth on the Eagle Mountain National Guard Base on June 7/8, 1958, but unfortunately, his result is not known.

Walt Cline, owner of thirty-five camera shops, had raced Corvettes until he was entered in the 450S for the race in Courtland, Alabama, on August 31, 1958. Cline won race 3 after 10 laps but had bad luck in race 5 as directly before the start of the race, the oil pressure suddenly dropped and #4510 would not start. Cline had other problems as reported in Willem Oosthoek's book about the 450S: "...his wife disliked motor racing intensely and all weekend trips with the 450S had to be planned with the highest secrecy. Cline's wife once found that her husband had entered a race with the Maserati and in a rage, she attacked the car – still being prepared in Harrison's shop – with a hammer, damaging its carburetors."

However, the next venue for Cline in #4510 was Dothan, Alabama, a tight circuit that did not fit the big 450S on October 25, 1958. In race 2 over 10 laps he was outgunned by E. D. Martin in his fast but smaller Ferrari 250TR and finished second overall. Cline could not finish in race 7 when the oil pipe of his Maserati broke.

The car remained unused by Harrison for the rest of the season. It reappeared in Coffeyville, Kansas on May 31, 1959. Perhaps Walt Cline's wife became the winner in their tough discussions about racing and he did not drive anymore. Jim Hall was behind the wheel of the car and gunned it to victory. He did it again at Courtland, Alabama, on October 11, 1959, in race 4 but in race 6 his Englebert tires gave up after 17 laps. He had to stop in the pits for replacements, then went back on the track, setting the fastest lap of the race. But he had lost too much time in the pits, finishing third behind E.D. Martin in his Ferrari 750 Monza and the winner Roy Schechter in his Porsche RSK. Almost two weeks later, on October 24, Hall in #4510 was in Dothan on Napier Field and did it again, winning race 3 over 8 laps and finishing second behind E.D. Martin in his Maserati Tipo 61 Birdcage. Race 9 saw the same results after 30 laps.

Nassau Speed Week in the Bahamas always attracted a lot of entrants. It was a welcome end to the season in warm weather and a pleasant atmosphere for socializing for all drivers. Harrison's team made the trip to these races on the Oakes field from November 31 to December 6, 1959. Jim Hall raced #4510 again with race number 97, while his own 450S that he had bought some months earlier was raced by Carroll Shelby with race number 98 (see the #4508 chapter). The big bonnet bulge, which was already larger than on the other cars, had become even larger at Nassau.

Hall finished the sprint race ninth overall but did better in the Governor's Trophy when he came home fifth. But in the main race, the prestigious Nassau Trophy, Hall crossed the finish line in twelfth place. The winner was George Constantine in an Aston Martin DBR2.

A long gap followed where the car remained unused. Harrison's team was in Elkhart Lake, Wisconsin for the Road America race. #4510 was driven only in practice by Jim Hall and Jim Jeffords and was then pulled away. It was the last race for #4510. It was driven again in Virginia in May 1961 for private practice by Fred Gamble who damaged the engine that would be replaced by engine 4514, purchased from the Maserati dealer, Rally Motors in New York. The Maserati was stored in Harrison's shop in Orange County, South California. In

Dan Clippenger took the brand-new #4510 for its first race in Chester in May 1958. Unused with the power of the big car, he spun but finally he was the first crossing the finish line. *(Michel Bollée Collection)*

Chief Stewart Prentice Knapp smiles to the camera before the race in Courtland in October 1959. *(Sam Houston)*

TOP AND OPPOSITE: After the race in Dothan in May 1959, #4510 gets finally uploaded into the truck and ready to be transported back to Dallas. *(Walter Bäumer Collection)*

The interior of #4510 in Dothan. Note the hand brake on its right. The gearlever had been modified and two additional gauges had mounded directly under the dashboard. *(Walter Bäumer Collection)*

OPPOSITE: Jim Hall with mechanic Bert Kemp (with hat) and some cool dudes at Coffeyville in May 1959 beside #4510. Note how Hall protected his right shoe from the chassis cross member beside the throttle. *(Bob Jackson)*

Chief mechanic Bert Kemp checks the rear of #4510 in the Coffeyville pitlane in May 1959. Note the fire distinguisher between the seats. It was Jim Hall's first race in the car and he crossed the finish line as the winner. *(Bob Jackson)*

Coffeyville in May 1959 was an easy win for Jim Hall in #4510. He had replaced Walt Cline as the driver for owner Frank Harrison. *(Bob Jackson)*

The starting grid of the race in Dothan in October 1959. Jim Hall in #4510 between the Roy Schechter's Porsche RSK and the new Maserati Tipo 61 Birdcage of E.D. Martin. Hall was the winner in Race C and Martin in Races 3 and 5 with Hall both as second. No. 23 is the Ferrari 250TR of Pete Harrison. *(Walter Bäumer Collection)*

OPPOSITE: Frank Harrison's mechanic Bert Kemp stands beside Jim Hall on the grid in Nassau in December 1959. In the sprint race, Hall could only finish as ninth overall and in the Governor's Trophy he came home as fifth. *(FORD Museum/Tom Friedman)*

In the main race, the Nassau Trophy, Jim Hall battles against Pedro Rodriguez in his Ferrari 250TR (10) and Allan Connell in his Ferrari 335S. Both Ferraris finished on thirteenth and tenth position while Hall was twelfth. It was not a successful Speed Week on the Bahamas for the young Texas racer. *(Walter Bäumer Collection)*

Charlie Lucas drove #4510 for its owner John Fellowes in a historic race in Le Mans in 1973. *(Walter Bäumer Collection)*

OPPOSITE: Dealer Bruce Vanyo had #4510 on the Orange County International Raceway, the home of Bob Bondurant's driving school of high-performance cars in California. *(Walter Bäumer Collection)*

256

Competition Press, in its March 31, 1962 issue, Harrison's mechanic Jerry Eisert, offered #4510 for sale, including a spare motor, via dealer Arciero Brothers on 140, East Whittier Boulevard in Montebello, California. But its owner then decided to use the car on public roads. For that reason, the car received disc brakes from a Corvette and a 4-speed gearbox. In 1968, Jerry Eisert sold the car for Harrison to Steve Hammatt from 16593 McLean Road, Mount Vernon, Washington for US$2,500, including its original brakes and gearbox.

Car Hunter, Colin Crabbe, owner of Antique Automobiles Ltd., Baston, near Peterborough, in England made an offer of US$4,000 to Hammatt who finally accepted US$5,000 for the car. In his book, *The Thrill of the Chase*, Crabbe wrote: "...Unbelievably, all the original parts were boxed up with the car so when back in the UK it was just a question of our workshops reassembling the Maserati. The car was raced by me and subsequently sold to John Fellowes, now Lord de Ramsey. [...] The Maserati 450S was driven in the 1972 Pomeroy Trophy at Silverstone attracting considerable attention due to its hair-raising acceleration. I won the standing quarter mile, so fast in fact that I was unable to stop the car until halfway down the Grand Prix circuit. Lunch was arranged [at a hotel, Ed.] later, so at full throttle and an almighty roar I passed the hotel at well over 100 mph and then braked to find there was nothing there. The brake pedal had broken clean off its mounting bracket, and it was a nasty moment since the car took ages to slow down enough before I could turn around to return, somewhat embarrassed. History had repeated itself as the 'Works' Maserati 450S had exactly the same problem during the 1957 Mille Miglia when Stirling Moss' brake pedal broke off causing the car to retire. [...] The brakes were not up to the power of the car even though the drums were enormous, and the handling left a lot to be desired when compared to a Maserati 300S of the same era."

John Fellowes, a member of the British Parliament and of the Maserati Club UK, commissioned a restoration of #4510 at the workshop of Trevor Stokes and then raced it in some historic events. In 1973, the car was entered by Fellowes in a historic race at Le Mans where it was driven by his friend, Charlie Lucas.

Dealer Bruce Vanyo from 2, Palo Alto Square in Palo Alto, California, became the new owner and sent it to Nino Epifani for restoration. Epifani drove the 450S in 1987 and 1988 in the historic Mille Miglia. On May 2, 1989, #4510 was sold by Christie's auction house in Monaco to Hans Thulin, an investor from Sweden, who drove it in the 1991 historic Mille Miglia where he over-revved the newly rebuilt engine. Unfortunately, the car had lost its two air intakes, a distinctive feature between the hood and the two front fenders on all later 450S.

Thulin's Swedish real estate empire collapsed in connection with the financial and real estate crash of the early 1990s. Upon Thulin's bankruptcy, the car was confiscated by Optima Bank of Sweden. This bank was also in financial trouble in 1992 and went bankrupt.

German nobleman Wendelin von Boch-Galhau, who was the CEO of the Villeroy & Boch porcelain empire, bought the car from Optima Bank and commissioned an engine rebuild by specialist Capricorn Engineering from Mönchengladbach in Germany. With the fresh engine, its owner drove it in August 1997 in the Oldtimer GP at the Nürburgring. On May 19, 1998, classic car dealer Klaus Werner from Wuppertal, Germany, bought the car and sent it back to Bruce Vanyo in California in September of that year who, in 1999, sold its to its current owner in Southern California.

Dealer Bruce Vanyo had #4510 on the Orange County International Raceway, the home of Bob Bondurant's driving school of high-performance cars in California. *(Walter Bäumer Collection)*

OPPOSITE: The current owner of #4510 had it on display at the Desert Spring Concours in 2013. *(Unknown photographer)*

4510 RACE HISTORY

16	May	1958	Chester, South Carolina, race 3	Dan Clippenger (no. 26) 1.OA
7/8	June	1958	Ft. Worth, Texas	Dan Clippenger (no. 26) result unknown
31	Aug.	1958	Courtland, Alabama, race 3	Walt Cline (no. 26) 1.OA
31	Aug.	1958	Courtland, Alabama, race 5	Walt Cline (no. 26) DNS
25	Oct.	1958	Dothan, Alabama, race 2	Walt Cline (no. 26) 2.OA
26	Oct.	1958	Dothan, Alabama, race 7	Walt Cline (no. 26) DNF
31	May	1959	Coffeyville, Kansas	Jim Hall (no. 126) 1.OA
11	Oct.	1959	Courtland, Alabama, race 4	Jim Hall (no. 26) 1.OA
11	Oct.	1959	Courtland, Alabama, race 6	Jim Hall (no. 26) 3.OA
24	Oct.	1959	Dothan, Alabama, race 3	Jim Hall (no. 26) 1.OA
25	Oct.	1959	Dothan, Alabama, race 6	Jim Hall (no. 26) 2.OA
25	Oct.	1959	Dothan, Alabama, race 9	Jim Hall (no. 26) 2.OA
04	Dec.	1959	Governor's Trophy, Nassau, Bahamas, Sprint	Jim Hall (no. 97) 9.OA
04	Dec.	1959	Governor's Trophy, Nassau, Bahamas	Jim Hall (no. 97) 5.OA
06	Dec.	1959	Nassau Trophy, Nassau, Bahamas	Jim Hall (no. 97) 12.OA
11	Sept.	1960	Road America, Elkhart Lake, Wisconsin	Jim Hall/Jim Jeffords (no. 26) DNS, practice only

4512 ex #4501/#4506

Completed: June 15, 1957
Engine: #4501, but later as GT car with engine #4512
Color: Red

The black Berlinetta Zagato coupé #4512 is a 1958 version of the red Le Mans coupé entered by the factory for the 24 Hours on June 22, 1957, modified for street use. It has a complicated story of chassis number swaps as happens sometimes with Maserati in that period when crossing a border outside Italy required customs documentation.

Stirling Moss became very important in the making of the car. In his book My Cars, My Career he wrote: "In 1957, I suggested that Maserati should build an aerodynamic-bodied coupé version of the 450S V8, primarily for Le Mans. I recommended Frank Costin, to design it since he had done such good work on those beautiful Lotus Elevens and on my Vanwall which was beginning to worry Maserati in Formula 1…. I think there was very little wrong with the design Frank produced for Maserati, but it just was diabolically badly made in a typically Italian last-minute panic. It was cramped, visibility was dreadful, it was unbearably hot, stuffy, and noisy, and we had to suffer all this on top of the normal 4.5 problems found in the open cars. I disliked Le Mans in any case, so all things considered that was not one of my favorite weekends…"

Since it was a last-minute decision and having no time to start the building of a new chassis from scratch, it was decided to take the new #4506 built for American John Edgar and redirect it to the construction of the Berlinetta coupé. Indeed, the factory-built sheet of #4506 states: "Changed number with 4501 provisionally." On the build sheets the engine number is written as #4506 and is then written over as #4501. The build sheet also lists the car as "Zagato 2 seats Berlinetta."

The Le Mans entries had already been completed and the chassis number 4501 specified on the customs paperwork. Since the ATA customs carnet 4501 was still valid after being used for the 1956 Kristianstad event (see the #4501 chapter) and Buenos Aires in 1957 (see #4503 chapter), the factory chose to renumber #4506 as #4501 to take advantage of the completed paperwork for the race. Moreover, the number 4501 was available because the original Kristianstad 450S prototype #4501 of 1956 was already dismantled and its

frame later restamped with number 3510, leaving the number 4501 available. Finally, because John Edgar had already been assigned number #4506, the 1957 Mille Miglia and Nürburgring 450S #4505 was renumbered to #4506, refreshed by the factory and sold to Edgar as a "new" car! (See #4505 and #4506 chapters.)

The Frank Costin-designed 450S Berlinetta was an oddly fantastic coupé. The bodywork was supposed to be done by Fantuzzi in Modena, but the coach builder had too much work and finally the plans and a mass of drawings went to Elio Zagato in Milan. It was four weeks before Le Mans. Moss: "…[Zagato] met their target date but cut so many corners to do so that when the car arrived at Le Mans, I could not believe the number of vital features omitted or fouled-up. One omission, for example, was the full-length undertray which Frank had specified in his original design!"

Another problem appeared when the Commission Sportive Internationale, C.S.I., refused to homologate the car with its transparent Perspex roof and two small sliding doors as on a fighter plane. The C.S.I. said it would be impossible to extract the driver if the car overturned. Costin rushed to Milan to modify his drawings. After many twists and turns, the car was ready just in time for Le Mans on June 15, 1957, but leaving no time to test it on the road. Hastily painted overnight, the car, road registered BO 66967, was loaded on the blue and yellow Fiat Bartoletti transporter with the other Maserati entries to arrive at Le Mans for scrutineering on Wednesday, June 19.

Nevertheless, the Maserati team was enthusiastic: "Its speed is 300 kph, everything has been thought about. A car like this is not affected by the weather…" claimed Bertocchi and Ugolini.

It was a very impressive car, and nothing had been seen like this in Le Mans before. Wherever it appeared during scrutineering, practice and behind the pits, the car, still numbered #4501, was the center of attention and surrounded by spectators who nicknamed it "Le Monstre." During the first practice session on

OPPOSITE: The boys at Zagato tried to do their best when building the coachwork that had been designed by Frank Costin, but they made it to their own taste and therefore made it wrong *(Unknown photographer)*

Moss examined #4512 with one of the factory mechanics after the car appeared in Le Mans in 1957. *(Walter Bäumer Collection)*

The car received much attention from the factory
mechanics at Le Mans. *(Bernard Cahier Archives)*

Stirling Moss with his friend Denis Jenkinson, watched by US driver Denise McCluggage, tries to modify a body panel to make it easier for him to drive. It quickly became clear that Zagato had changed the design of the car provided by Costin in such a way that, among other problems, there was hardly any cooling for the driver in the interior. Note Moss' traveling bag with all the airline stickers on it. *(Bernard Cahier Archives)*

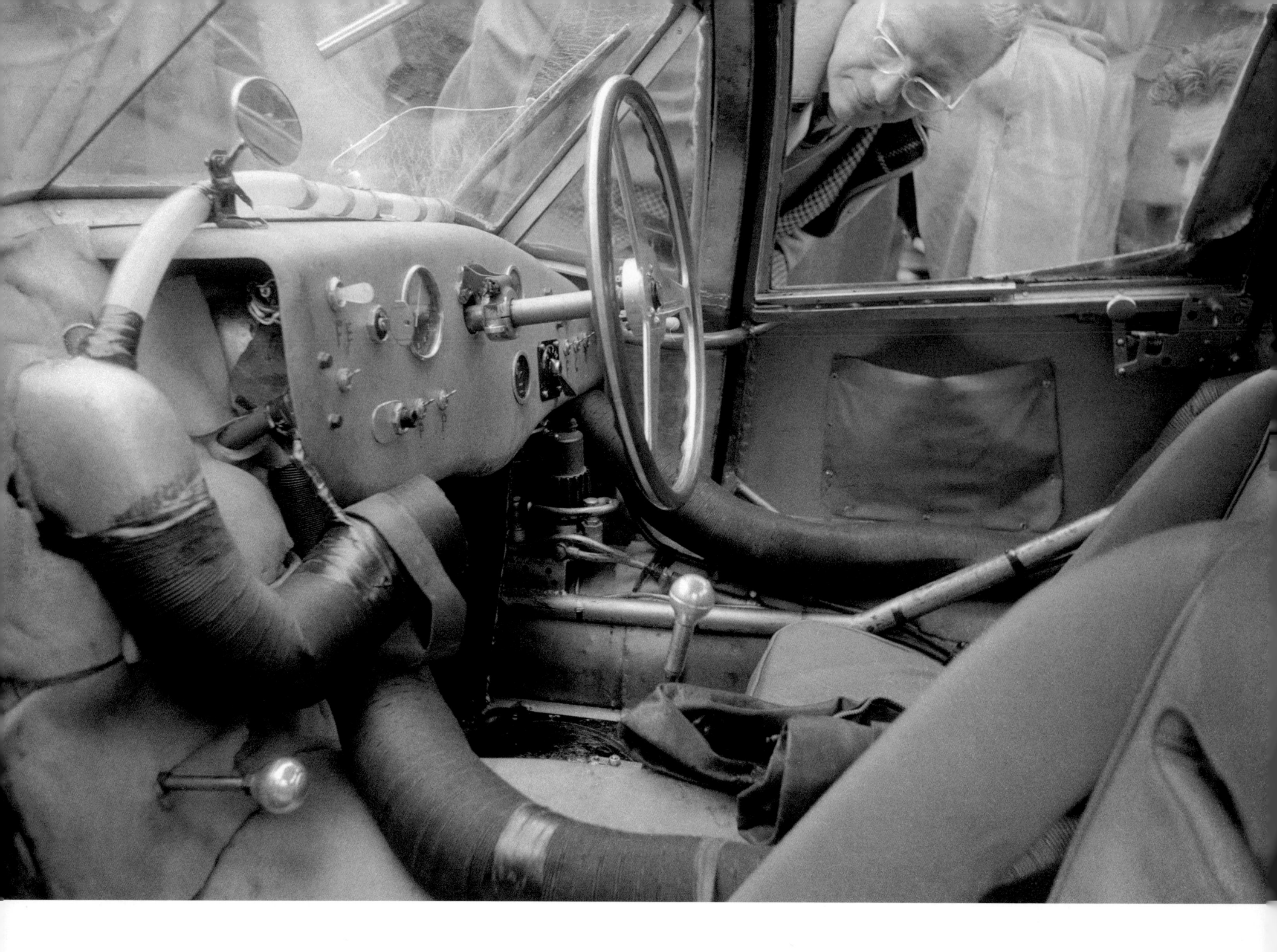

An improvised arrangement of hoses was installed in the driver's compartment to draw cooler air from the outside. *(Klemantaski Collection)*

OPPOSITE: Wherever the car appeared in Le Mans, it was the center of attention. It was a car never seen before in that legendary long-distance race. Note the fuel filler cap in the rear window and the small rectangular air vents. *(Klemantaski Collection)*

Coming back from night practice at Le Mans, Moss complained about the disappointing performance of #4512. *(Walter Bäumer Collection)*

OPPOSITE: Moss tried his best to catch up to the leading cars and had just overtaken the Ferrari 250TR of Olivier Gendebien and Maurice Trintignant. Neither car saw the finish line. *(Walter Bäumer Collection)*

A great photograph that shows the magic of Le Mans in the 1950s. Everybody on the pit grandstand looked at #4512 while some mechanics try to keep the car in the race. *(David Wright/Brian Joscelyne)*

Wednesday evening, Moss and Harry Schell almost suffocated in the cockpit due to heat radiation and lack of ventilation. Moss: "...In practice [...] it was slower than the normal open 4.5. [...] We worked hard to cool its cockpit. We fitted windscreen wipers – it had been completed without any – but the airflow blew them clear off the screen. They would just make contact sufficient to smear the screen as we braked, and then lift clear again to quiver in the airstream as we built up speed, leaving us peering through the smeared screen. The lights were poor, and the throttle jammed. I was not happy..."

When Maserati mechanics cut several holes in the bodywork to provide cockpit cooling, any benefit from Costin's airflow concept was lost as it was also missing the full-length undertray which Costin had specified in his original design. But not only that, the cooling air supply to the carburetor system planned by Costin was missing and so the engine could only rev up to maximum 6,200rpm, instead of 7,000rpm of the barchetta.

The best lap time in practice at Le Mans was recorded by Juan Manuel Fangio in the 450S, #4503 race number 2 while Moss with the Zagato coupé race number 1 scored the fourth best lap after two Ferraris.

The race day was the beginning of a nightmare for Moss and Schell: the red coupé lost its small windshield bonnet in the first lap; then its heat shields around the exhaust system. On the long, straight road in Les Hunaudières the speed did not exceed 270 kph; severe vibrations also affected roadholding, making it very loose. The four-part windshield seriously impaired visibility and the drivers still suffered from intense heat and fumes in the cockpit. Moss performed miracles running in second place after two hours behind Behra's 450S.

But it was a short success as a dehydrated Moss soon returned to the pits complaining of vibrations from the transmission and unbearable heat in the cockpit despite the windows being wide open. Schell re-entered the race but five laps later, the big coupé came back in with a trail of smoke. A broken oil pipe was repaired, and Moss returned to the race. A few laps later, the Costin-Zagato 450S coupé retired with a broken transmission. Stirling Moss concluded in his memoir: "In the final reckoning, the 4.5 coupé was more Zagato than Costin, and the poor quality of Zagato's work against the clock, combined with Maserati 4.5's usual shortcomings, was more that we could stand... I have no regrets about never having driven that car again."

The 1957 24 Hours of Le Mans was the only race for the Zagato coupé which returned to Modena and was ingloriously consigned to Maserati's scrap heap at the factory premises, having lost its engine and Borrani wheels.

The Mulsanne straight, also called "Les Hunaudières", was the fastest part of the Le Mans circuit. Although #4512 was slower than the Barchetta, the sound of these cars here must have been incredible. *(Motorsportimages.com)*

The 24 Hours of Le Mans were over for Maserati and #4512 is packed up ready to leave. *(Duane Kinslow)*

A fuzzy photograph that shows #4512 stored in the factory scrapyard. In the back is the stunning coachwork of the A6GCS Pininfarina coupé, #2057. *(Trident)*

Swiss journalist and part time wheeler-dealer Hans Tanner discussed the engine of #4512 with Maserati chief mechanic Guerino Bertocchi after the car had resumed a second life in a stunning black color with Byron Staver. *(Walter Bäumer Collection)*

OPPOSITE: Another photograph of Hans Tanner with Guerino Bertocchi, probably taken before Tanner test drove the car. The multi-part front screen from Le Mans had been replaced by a single GT screen. *(Walter Bäumer Collection)*

#4512 in the USA and displayed at the New York Auto Show in 1962. The car is now painted red. *(Walter Bäumer Collection)*

In 1970, this photograph was sent by dealer Walter Weimer to a potential buyer of the car. *(Walter Bäumer Collection)*

In late 1957, Temple Buell, the owner of #4508, had expressed an interest in the big coupé, but Maserati was reluctant to build a GT car because of the noise produced by the rear-mounted gearbox differential which was even noisier than the 4.5-liter V8 engine itself. Instead, Buell bought an exclusive prototype 3500GT cabriolet by Touring, one of only two made.

One year later the Zagato coupé came back to life. In April 1958, two Americans from Minnesota, Byron Staver and his son John, visited the factory in Modena. Noticing the abandoned big coupé, Byron Staver commissioned Maserati to convert it into a Grand Turismo car for road use. Giulio Alfieri designed new and quieter gears and the coupé received a complete makeover: to increase the cockpit space for the tall Staver. Fantuzzi worked on the frame and stretched it by 25 cm right through the middle which led to wider doors. A wrap-around windshield replaced the original four-piece version and functional rear quarter windows were added for visibility and ventilation. A huge flap at the rounded rear could be opened to provide access to the spare wheel.

The modified Zagato body also received front vents under the headlights, large chrome side vents to evacuate the hot air from the engine and a chromed mesh over the dual side exhaust pipes. The original 4.5-liter V8 engine was refitted and claimed 380HP because of smaller 45 IDM Weber carbs. Inside the car, the steering went from right to left-hand drive and a 3500GT dashboard was installed with a grab bar. New brown leather upholstery finished the fancy interior. The sleek upgraded coupé without bumpers was painted a spectacular bright black and its radiator air intake received an aluminum surround with a 3500GT Trident in its oval.

The black coupé was renumbered 4512 and described as very comfortable by journalist Hans Tanner after a test drive with Guerino Bertocchi. Photographer Jesse Alexander was there and took a series of shots in the courtyard of the factory. Byron Staver paid US$12,000 and the car was shipped to New York where he collected it early in September 1958 and drove it cross-country to Minnesota. Then Staver used his black coupé registered 8H 7598 for road trips to Chicago and Texas where the coupé was serviced in Dallas at Yale Boulevard in the workshop of Jim Hall. Mechanic Frank Lance remembered that Guerino Bertocchi himself tuned the Webers when he made a stopover in Dallas after taking care of Buell's 250F cars in Australia in January 1959. Byron Staver covered a total of 2,000 highway miles but complained that the noise level over 50mph "made this car more suited to a track than the highway."

Then Staver put the coupé up for sale via Chicago-based exotic car dealer Harry Woodnorth and in the December 1958 issue of *Sportscar magazine* it was offered for US$17,000. Unsold at this price, the coupé was back in the magazine one year later in December 1959: "'58 Maserati, 4.5 Coupé, ex-Moss Le Mans car, 9,500$." It took Woodnorth another year to sell #4512 at the annual Sports Car Show in late 1960 at the Ford Museum in Detroit to Harry Heinl of 4401 Lagrange Street in Toledo, Ohio. Interestingly, the car had also been offered for sale by dealer, Thoroughbred Car Co., at 820 North Broadway in the newspaper *The Daily Oklahoman* in the May 30 1959 issue. The new owner brought the coupé, newly registered 4512M in Ohio, to Frank

Harrison in Chattanooga, Tennessee for evaluation where Harrison's mechanic Bert Kemp did an engine revision and a transmission overhaul: new bearings, ring and pinion gears were installed. But on the way back to Toledo, Heinl had a broken valve shattering a piston while driving in downtown Cincinnati. The car was returned to Harrison's shop for the engine work to be done all over again. A new hood panel was refabricated as the original one from Le Mans was unrestorable after having been cut and patched so much that it could not stand one more refurbish.

With the engine out, Harry Heinl changed the colors of his car, and the black coupé was painted a '55 Buick red, while the leather upholstery changed from brown to black. All the vent holes which had been seen on the car at Le Mans were found, filled in under the stripped black paint. Heinl placed a for sale advertisement in *The New York Times* on August 7, 1960, and in *Competition Press* on June 30, and December 8, 1962.

The now red coupé received national coverage in the *Road & Track* issue of March 1963 with ten photographs in a six-page feature "Costin-Maserati Le Mans Coupé." Enthusiastic reporter, Warren Fitzgerald, concluded: "I have never, I repeat never, had such an automotive experience as I had photographing, listening to, and riding in this fabulous machine." Two months later, on May 1963, the Zagato coupé made the cover of *Car and Driver* magazine after it had been awarded class winner at the Concours d'Elégance of the 1963 New York International Show.

Then there was a succession of several American owners after Harry Heinl; Charles Kilgore in New York in 1964, Bob Morgan in New Jersey via dealer Bob Grossman, then it was sold to Walter Weimer who lived at 712 Whitehall Road, Washington, Pennsylvania. In 1968, he commissioned an engine overhaul by Reg Hallums. Weimer offered the car for sale in a letter dated December 21, 1969, to Dick Merrit, who was from New York. Weimer also offered it in April and May 1970 in *Autoweek*, in restored condition, asking US$12,500.

The next owner was Pete Sherman from 190 Shell Point West, Maitland, Florida, who offered it in 1973 in a small advertisement: "This 220mph is considered by many to be the most famous modern sports car in the world. Stored indoors last five years. $22,500 or exotic trade."

The Zagato coupé was sold in March 1973 to Jim Rodgers in Tennessee and restored by Holman-Moody in North Carolina. Then during the US Grand Prix at Watkins Glen in October 1976 the car was reunited with Stirling Moss who commented: "It is far more attractive now than I remember it."

In 1978, the car left the USA to return to Europe, to Aschaffenburg, Germany. Peter Kaus, collector and owner of the famous Rosso Bianco collection displayed it in his museum and kept it until 2002 when he sold it to collector Alfredo Brenner from Houston, Texas. The new owner commissioned the Italian dealer Franco Meiners from Bergamo to coordinate a full restoration. The Zagato coupé was entirely returned to its original appearance when it left Italy in 1958 with Byron Staver: a stunning black with brown leather upholstery. The black coupé was shown in 2004

#4512 today and back in black before being auctioned by Sotheby's in about 2000. *(Unknown photographer)*

in Villa d'Este Concours d'Elegance and Le Mans Classic, bearing the old factory registration BO 66967, and then shipped to Brenner's home in Texas.

Finally, the black Zagato coupé was sold in June 2007 via the Ferrari dealer Onofrio Triarsi of Florida to an important American collector. Expert Dyke Ridgley, who handles the car for its owner, wrote in November 2012 to one of the authors: "The engine in 4512, the Zagato coupé is a mix of parts. The left cylinder head is #1, the right cylinder head is from engine #5 and the engine number stamping is 4512, though you can easily see where it has been stamped over older numbers. When Maserati rebuilt the car for Byron Staver, they used the project to profitably use up a number of 450S spares."

In the later years, Chassis 4512 was shown in the Pebble Beach Concours d'Elégance Beach in California and Cavallino Classic in Florida.

4512 RACE HISTORY (as #4501)

| 22-23 | June | 1957 | 24 Hours of Le Mans | Stirling Moss/Harry Schell (no. 1) DNF |

4203 "Eldorado"

Completed: June 16, 1958
Color: white

This Maserati Monoposto was built in 1958 to take part in the "Trophy of Two Worlds" raced on the ring part of the Monza circuit.

The Italian Federation's idea was to pit the best single-seaters from the New World, the United States with their Indy Formulas, against the best single-seaters of the Old World, Europe with its Formula 1 racers, in a single race over 500 Miles.

In 1957 the event had taken place on the ring at Monza, and was the first time where the Americans, without much European opposition, had won with Jimmy Bryan in a Dean Van Lines Special, an Indy roadster with Offenhauser engine and Kuzma chassis. In June 1958, the Europeans wanted to take their revenge and hired their best teams: three single-seater Ferraris for Luigi Musso, Phil Hill and Harry Schell, two Jaguar D-Types for Masten Gregory and Ivor Bueb, one Lister for Jack Fairman and finally one single-seater Maserati for Stirling Moss: the "Eldorado-Italia". Argentinian champion Juan Manuel Fangio came out of his recent retirement to compete on the Dean Van Lines winner of the previous year.

Under the auspices and finances of Gino Zanetti, the Italian king of Eldorado ice cream, Maserati was asked to build a car with which to participate in the Monza 500 Miles. Zanetti thought that motor sport competition was the ideal stage to promote his brand and product throughout the world. After being sponsored by pasta manufacturer Buitoni for the 1957 Mille Miglia, the deal between Zanetti and Maserati was the first example of big modern sponsorship by a brand not related to the motoring world.

Engineer Giulio Alfieri developed a single-seater, a hybrid car equipped with a 450S V8 engine reduced to 4.2 liters, a solid original chassis, brakes from the 250F and bodywork by Maserati's official coachbuilder, Medardo Fantuzzi.

The 400hp engine was in offset position by 9cm to the left side, which allowed the transmission shaft to pass next to the driver and under the oil tank. The gearbox had only 2 speeds: start, roll, and full speed! With Indianapolis-type

Hallibrand magnesium wheels and Firestone tires the whole machine had a curb weight of only 758 kg. Stirling Moss was hired as driver and Carroll Shelby from the USA as his backup.

The Americans dominated in the tests with their roadsters equipped with the powerful Offenhauser 4.2-liter 4-cylinder engine. Stirling Moss qualified the Eldorado in the middle of the grid and only another European driver was better: the Ferrari 412 V12-4.1-liter with 420hp, driven by the heroic Luigi Musso who climbed to pole position at an average of 281 km/h to the greatest happiness of the Italian *Tifosi*! Fangio, officially retired from racing but still in good shape, achieved the third best time but was not on the starting grid due to a damaged piston in the Offy engine of his car.

The 500 Mile race was scheduled in three heats of 63 laps each, due to tire wear and ambient heat. In the first heat, Moss, cautious at the start, joined in the fight between Bob Veith and Bill Ward at the head of the race. The Eldorado finished fourth and was the fastest European car. In the second heat, Moss, distanced at the start, pulled out all the stops and advanced to second place, but at the end of the race degraded tires forced him to let his American rivals, Jimmy Bryan, Bob Veith and Troy Ruttman slip away; Moss finally finished fifth overall.

In the third and final round, gearbox problems slowed Moss down, then well back, the steering broke on lap 44 and sent the Eldorado against the protection rails of the south curve: the car spun several times to finish at the bottom of the track. Moss was not injured but the Eldorado was out of the race. Later Moss would write that he opened his eyes and found to his surprise that he was not dead! The Maserati finished seventh overall in the three races with 164 laps covered. Without its retirement it would have been in third place. Luigi Musso's Ferrari was the best European overall, in third place behind Jimmy Bryan's Belond and the victorious Jim Rathmann in the Zink Leader Card with a Watsons chassis.

Gino Zanetti was nevertheless happy with his promotion and chose to repair the car. The Eldorado was re-bodied without the rear fin and repainted red to

Maserati chief mechanic Guerino Bertocchi drove some test laps in Monza. The car had the traditional headrest which proved not to be effective at higher speeds. *(Jean-Pierre Lasartigues Collection)*

In the 1950s, Gino Zanetti was the "King of Ice Cream" in Italy. He financed the unique single-seater for Maserati. Painted in white it promoted the name of his leading ice cream brand. The first roll-out of the car was at Monza where Zanetti talked with Stirling Moss about the car. *(Unknown photographer)*

OPPOSITE: Moss prepares for the practice session at Monza prior to the Trophy of Two Worlds race at Monza 1958.
(Jean-Pierre Lasartigues Collection)

Bertocchi checks the spark plugs of the car in Monza. Note the two big magnetos on the front end of the engine. *(Revs Institute)*

The car was modified with a more efficient, long aerodynamic fin on its rear end. *(Klemantaski Collection)*

Moss high up in the banking of Monza, between the Jaguar D-Type of Ivor Bueb and the 4.1 Ferrari 412MI of Mike Hawthorn who finished the race third overall. *(Klemantaski Collection)*

OPPOSITE: Moss was on lap 44 and in fourth place, when something went wrong with the steering. The car went out of control, hit the steel Armco high in the banking and two tires blew out. Moss became only a passenger when the car careened down the infield. Moss escaped unhurt but the car was severely damaged. *(Bernard Cahier Archives)*

After the crash in Monza, the car was repaired and modified. It appeared in the USA for the Indy 500 in May 1959, repainted red. Also, the rear fin from Monza was removed. Driver Ralph Liguori was not able to qualify for the race. *(Revs Institute)*

be entered the following year in the 500 Miles of Indianapolis in the USA. Zanetti hired two Maserati mechanics plus chief mechanic, Guerino Bertocchi, and they arrived at Indianapolis on May 8,1959. The car was entrusted to the driver Ralph Liguori who failed to qualify for the race. Now Zanetti had had enough. The Eldorado returned to Modena and was stored indefinitely in a corner of the Maserati factory.

Sixteen years later, in 1975, after the Argentinian Alessandro de Tomaso had purchased the Maserati factory with the help of the Italian government, the Eldorado was entrusted to the Carrozzeria Campana in Modena for restoration to its 1958 Monza configuration. Following the sale of Maserati to Ferrari in the late 1990s, the Eldorado became part of the Panini collection in Modena, exhibited alongside other historic Maserati cars.

Chassis #4203 "Eldorado" with its owner on the iced lake of St. Moritz in Switzerland very early in 2023. *(Maserati S.p.A.)*

4203 "Eldorado" RACE HISTORY

29 June 1958	Trophy of Two Worlds, Monza	Stirling Moss (no. 10) 7 O.A
30 May 195	Indy 500, Indianapolis, Indiana	Ralph Liguori (no. 12) DNQ

In 1984, experienced historic racer Willie Green, who drove almost every car type dating from prewar years to the 1970s, took out chassis #4506 at Silverstone for a track test for the UK-magazine *Classis & Sportscar*. He reported in the August 1984 issue:

"This track test was one of those moments of sheer opportunism which began, in time-honored fashion, over a beer. One evening I was chatting to restorer Stephen Griswold when the subject of his latest restoration came up; before I knew it, I had been invited to drive what is probably the most powerful front-engined sports racing car ever. I had to present myself at Silverstone the next day …

The reason for the rush was that this very special Maserati 450S, with its 6.4-litre 'marine' engine, was due to be dispatched to its [then, Ed.] owner, Peter Kaus, as soon as Griswold had given it a clean bill of health. That meant a shakedown session at Silverstone, where I would have the chance of a few laps during the day. My first impression once I'd strapped myself in was that the seating position was very low, and that the car looked huge and heavy to handle. On the move, though, I found that the controls were quite light, but I disliked the upright seat and the wooden steering wheel rim, which was so slippery that you could inadvertently let go of it. One interesting detail I noticed as I was checking round the cockpit before driving off was a small peephole behind my right shoulder so

that you could check the tire wear during a race. A necessary tweak, I thought, imagining all the power that would have gone through the rear wheels with the ordinary 4.5-litre V8 of its heyday, let alone this 6.4-litre monster.

As I expected, the handling was neutral until I put my boot in — that just destroyed it. You would set up the car in the middle of a corner at, say, 3,000 rpm, put the welly in, and the back end would just go. It was not as if the tail suddenly stepped sideways a little: the immediate wheelspin meant that the effect was far more dramatic than that. Coming out of Woodcote, it felt as if the rear wheels didn't start to bite properly until halfway down the pits straight. I would say that there's around 400-450bhp available (Steve agreed that it's in that

region), but the incredible torque is the most striking characteristic. Although the engine is red-lined at 5700rpm, the torque seems to peak at around 3,000, and you don't need much more than 4,000 anywhere at Silverstone.

I'm not sure whether this kind of power is more than the chassis can handle, but it was certainly more than the driver could in this instance. Power is way in excess of roadholding because of the narrow tires, and now I think about it, there are very few racing cars which push so much power through so little rubber. I can't imagine what it would have been like to drive a pre-war Mercedes-Benz or Auto Union! Mind you, I think the 450S could have done with different tires: this one was all wrong because there was more rubber on the front than the back.

The gearing was very high, good for 185mph in fifth. I should say, I never got into fifth, even though I was changing at 4,000rpm. I had been told to expect a noisy gearbox, but I didn't find it so. I used only the middle three gears, but I reckon I could have gone just as quickly with only third and fourth. It reminded me, in fact, of the Can Am McLaren I drove, for that also had so much torque that the gears were almost a luxury! The linkage fell off when I drove the McLaren, so I had to leave it in top, and I went 2 seconds a lap quicker. The brakes are adequate for the power but felt as if they were fading out through lack of hydraulic travel. And the old bugbear of driving a car like this in an open test session cropped up. All and sundry were out on the track, and some of those little heroe — making no allowance for the fact that I was driving a ton of uncontrollable machinery — did odd things like drive round the outside of me through a corner, which isn't wise when the car is in the middle of a great opposite-locking power slide …

When I came in after only about 10 minutes in the car I knew that I'd been driving quite a handful: I wasn't exhausted, but I would have been after half an hour. It was like fighting a battleship. This time I didn't envy the car's owner, who was due to do the Mille Miglia in it. I wouldn't have set out over 1,000 miles without a team of 20 drivers!

Obviously, this car has more power than the 1957 team cars ever knew, and they were the most powerful sports racers of their day. Latterly I can remember Charlie Lucas having a good old go in John Fellowes' 450S, but I can now understand why John never drove very quickly. Driving one in the dry is a bit like coping with any other rear-driven racing car in the wet…"

And 20 years later, on a cold morning, UK Journalist Paul Fearnley tested chassis #4502 on the old Nürburgring. He wrote in *Motor Sport* in the January 2005 issue:

"…The woodland creatures scurry, bolt, and scramble, for the "Bazooka", though still some way distant, is most definitely within earshot. This is not a car for the shy or sensitive, timid or tremulous. Genghis Khan or Vlad the Impaler would have loved it, though. Maserati's Tipo 54, that's Mister 450S to you and me, sounds like thunder and goes like the clappers. It has a preference for straights, swallowing them whole, but is allergic to corners. It's big, beautiful, and brutal...

OPPOSITE: Chassis #4502 was driven by Willie Green for the UK magazine *Classic & Sportscar* in 1984. (*Classic & Sportscar*)

Chassis #4502 driven by chief editor Paul Fearnley on the Nürburgring for his feature in the January 2005-issue of the UK magazine *Motor Sport*. (*Walter Bäumer*)

"...The 450S is augmented and outrageous and draws gawping crowds. Onlookers take a few paces back when its 4.5-litre 90-degree V8 Richters into life, but they can't tear themselves away. The 450S is a hero's car: upfront and usually out front, incomprehensible and unforgiving, stupidly fast and – even in the hands of a Moss or a Fangio – downright dangerous. This is not a car that puts a comforting arm around you. Instead, it grabs you by the throat and challenges you to an arm wrestle. It looks big from without and feels big from within. You sit low in its wide cockpit and grasp a three-spoke wooden steering wheel that's set a tad high for my taste.

"Sports racers of the 1950s are usually cramped; I feel swamped in this. And daunted by that engine. Circling and surveying the car as it was warmed-up, I'd convinced myself that each bank had a different note: left pipe a background hint of high hat, right pipe the thud of bass drum. The stereo effect once in the driving seat, however, generates a towering wall of sound, menacing at tickover, otherworldly on the hoof. There are, though, some crumbs of comfort: the clutch is light and Valerio Colotti's transaxle is a joy, short of throw, deliberate of action. This is a five-speed box as opposed to the four of most [Maserati] 300Ss, and it is sited ahead of the final drive whereas the 300S had its transmission to the right of the diff. Clearly, it's too simplistic to state that the 450S is a beefed-up version of its 3-litre predecessor but think of it that way and you won't go far wrong. It retains, for instance, a coil sprung wishbone front and transverse-leaf-sprung de Dion rear.

"The first shock comes at the first corner. Travelling at no great speed I attempt to swing in – and nothing happens. The first quarter-turn of what should be lock appears to be play, at which point everything loads up and the nose grudgingly comes around. Okay, so you drive it on the throttle. But at this point you are entering Moss territory – and even he reckoned it a handful. Hmm. Then there's the brakes. They are masterpieces of the casting art, all fins and radial holes drilled at an angle to improve cooling. Clay cold today, they feel dead and grabby...

"...A bit of heat would improve things but I can categorically state that they are not up to the job. How? Simply because this much grunt and torque would test far more modern set-ups. Cracking open the throats of the four downdraught Webers nestling down in the vee causes a supercar-like surge of urge. Snapping them open causes wheelspin in second and third – in the dry, on the uphill rush to the Karussell-section [of the old Nürburgring]. I can't drive like Moss, but I grin like him. And then the tail steps out through the gentlest of rights after the Karussell and I go all serious again.

And that's just 5,400rpm (in only second gear) according to the telltale; 1,600 revs still to go. I'm simply blown away. And that's with fifth gear still marooned and unused out on its dogleg. This is one fearsome reputation that is fully deserved. It briefly crosses my mind that Moss might have spent the night before his Mille Miglia 'disappointment' stealthily part-sawing through the brake shaft with a nail file. His effort to lead the 'Ring 1,000 'Clicks' in a 450S was Herculean..."

THE PERSONALITIES

Guerino Bertocchi

As a twenty-one-year-old mechanic, Guerino Bertocchi was Alfieri Maserati's co-driver in his Tipo 26 in the 1926 Targa Florio. He was the chief mechanic of Officine Maserati from the beginning and a member of the works team in all major events pre- and postwar, and participated in some Mille Miglia races as co-driver. He became famous all over Italy and was highly respected. His word was the law in the Maserati racing department that included his brother Gino Bertocchi, and the mechanics: Arturo Brancolini, Giorgio Neri, Manni and Giulio Borsari in the pitlanes of all the circuits. Bertocchi knew all the drivers, including Nuvolari, Zehender, Dreyfus, Varzi, Borzacchini, Campari, Moss, Behra, Perdisa and Schell, during the long racing tradition of the company, and guided them through their careers under the Maserati banner. Fangio only stepped into a car that had been given the final check by Bertocchi. As a test driver he drove all the racing cars built by the factory on the Aerautodromo in Modena and was an expert on that circuit. He stayed with Maserati when the Orsi family sold the company to Citroën in the late 1960s and was well known among customers for his fearless drives demonstrating the GT cars. In 1971, he left the factory and started work for Alessandro de Tomaso's company. Guerino Bertocchi died in an accident co-driving a De Tomaso GT car in 1981, too soon to write a book about his amazing adventures in the world of racing.

Jean Behra

Born in 1921 in Nice, Behra began his racing career on motorcycles. He became the main works driver for the Paris-based company of Amédée Gordini. In 1955, he signed his contract with Maserati as the number one driver and was closely involved with the development of the 300S. He became the backbone of the Maserati factory team both in sports car and Grand Prix racing. He was fast, aggressive, and reliable behind the wheel, but was a charming person when he stepped out of the car. His biggest success was the win in the 1956 1,000 km Nürburgring with Moss, Taruffi and Schell with a 300S, and at the 1957 12 Hours of Sebring with Fangio in the 450S. Winning both the 12 Hours of Sebring and the Swedish Grand Prix, Behra was the most successful factory driver in the 450S. His trademark attire was a red polo shirt and white helmet with a checkered band. After Maserati withdrew from racing in 1957, he joined the BRM team and later signed with Ferrari in 1959. Very loyal to Maserati, he had difficulties with Ferrari and the politics in Maranello. Tragically he met his fate driving a Porsche at the Avus on August 1, 1959, when he crashed against an old Flak tower on top of the banking.

Juan Manuel Fangio

Much has been written about this most famous of racing drivers. He was the Master. Born on July 24, 1911 in Argentina, Fangio drove in some prewar races in South America, and went to Europe in the late 1940s with the support of Juan Perón. His first race appearance was with a Simca-Gordini at the Reims GP in 1948, and then with a Maserati 4CLT at Palermo in 1949. The next year he drove for Alfa Romeo, and in 1951 became the Formula 1 World Champion. 1954 saw his second Championship when he was first under contract with Maserati but changed mid-season to Mercedes-Benz. The following year he was again World Champion driving exclusively with Mercedes before he moved to Ferrari in 1956, finishing that season with his fourth Championship. Back with Maserati one year later, he achieved his fifth title in his epic drive in a Tipo 250F on the Nürburgring. More successful in single-seaters, he also had some great wins in sports car races with Lancia, Mercedes, Ferrari and Maserati. His smooth driving style coupled with his ability to almost always find that extra second to be faster than everyone else made him the absolute Number One on the Maserati team, and indeed with all the other marques. Fangio signed a contract with Maserati only for Formula 1 engagements in 1957 but was helping out in the 450S as well. He retired from racing in 1958. Highly respected and a legend in the racing world, he died in 1995.

Nello Ugolini

Born near Modena in 1906, Nello Ugolini had a passion for soccer and motor sport. From 1932 to 1939, he was a secretary to Enzo Ferrari in his Scuderia. During World War II, he worked for Alfa Romeo and was a director of the Italian soccer teams in the late 1940s. He returned to Ferrari in 1952 as racing director. In 1956, Ugolini, who was always respectfully called "Maestro," became team manager for all Maserati racing activities. His greatest success was winning the 1957 Formula 1 World Championship for the company. He brilliantly handled the great win in Sebring in 1957 with Fangio/Behra in a 450S, and many more. Ugolini was also the man from whom wealthy gentlemen drivers could buy the team cars after the races. Nello Ugolini died in 2000.

Masten Gregory

He always looked like a big boy in the racing scene. Born in 1932, he wore large glasses due to his bad eyesight. In 1955, he was the first driver for Tony Parravano's team, driving his 300S. Later he changed to the "team" of Temple Buell and crashed spectacularly in Buell's 450S in Caracas in 1957. He drove all sorts of racing cars and was also successful in Europe. In 1957, he won the 1,000 km of Buenos Aires in a Ferrari. His biggest success was to win the 1965 24 Hours of Le Mans together with Jochen Rindt in a Ferrari 250LM. He retired from the sport in 1972 and stayed in Europe, where he died in 1985 in his home in Italy.

Stirling Moss

Moss drove almost every type of race car in his tremendous career but became synonymous with the 300S and nobody had more races and achieved so much success with this car. His greatest races with Maserati sports cars were in the 1956 editions of the 1,000 km of Buenos Aires, the 1,000 km of Nürburgring, and in the 1957 12 Hours of Sebring, where he came second overall in a 300S. He became a legend initially by winning the 1955 Mille Miglia with Denis Jenkinson for Mercedes-Benz, and joined the Maserati works team the next year as the number one driver for both sports cars and single seaters. He moved to Vanwall in 1957 but stayed with Maserati for the sports car entries, always preferring the 300S over the much more powerful 450S for which he had a lot of respect. Of all the ten 450S made, he alone drove six cars including the notorious prototype that was based on his unlucky 350S.

His numerous wins with Formula 1 and sports cars of all kinds made him one of the best-known drivers worldwide. He retired from racing in 1962 when he crashed badly in his Lotus-Climax at Goodwood. He became a motor sport legend by himself and died in 2020.

Carroll Shelby

Born in 1923 in Leesburg, Texas, Carroll Shelby became a professional race driver in 1954. He was famous for his striped bib overalls and funny hats. Shelby became associated with John Edgar, who ran a stable of high-class Ferrari and Maserati racing cars and was kept busy driving Edgar's 300S and 450S. He was extremely successful, and in 1956 was named "Sports Car Driver of the Year" by Sports Illustrated. With Jim Hall, he ran a Maserati dealership in Texas for a while. Shelby later raced the 450S for Temple Buell. He next turned his attention to Europe where he drove for Scuderia Centro Sud in Formula 1 races and had his biggest international racing success winning the 1959 24 Hours of Le Mans with Roy Salvadori for Aston Martin. In 1960, he withdrew from racing for health reasons and became the creator of the famous Cobra cars which challenged Ferrari. A legend in his own right, Carroll Shelby was a familiar sight at many US automobile events, and he established the Carroll Shelby Children's Foundation to help indigent children with heart or kidney problems. He died in 2012.

Bill Krause

Born in 1933, Bill Krause started his racing career driving midgets on California oval dirt tracks. He went on to race his own Jaguar D-Type, which he later converted to Chevrolet Corvette power. He became synonymous with the 450S owned by Jack Brumby and Rey Martinez and drove the car in eight events. Of his many races, Krause believes that his most memorable win was at the 1962 Pomona Road Races where he drove Steve Diulo's Maserati Tipo 61 Birdcage. Later, he also drove Cobras for Shelby who considered him the best US driver of that time. Krause raced at Riverside 20 times, Santa Barbara 14 times, and also at Pomona, Laguna Seca and more. He retired from motor racing in the mid-1960s and opened both a Honda motorcycle and automobile dealership in California. He lives today in Indian Wells, California.

John Edgar

John Edgar was born in 1902 in a wealthy family that owned the Hobart Manufacturing company and became a true race fanatic and car enthusiast. Driving MGs in the beginning, he turned his interest to Ferrari in the early 1950s and then to a Porsche 550. His drivers were Ernie McAfee and Bill Pollack. Edgar always enjoyed himself, no matter what, and he became the biggest supporter of the Riverside racetrack. He bought a big Ferrari 857S and 410S and his silver truck to transport the race cars was famous for years. His main driver was Carroll Shelby who drove his Maserati 300S and then the 450S in many races. After a full life of fun and show, he died in Beverly Hills in 1972.

Jim Hall

Born in 1935 in Texas, he had one of the most remarkable race careers of all American drivers. First competing in an Allard in 1953, he drove almost everything that was fast. He raced OSCA, Ferrari and started his activities with cars from Maserati in a 200S. Carroll Shelby was his mentor for his first race in a 450S in 1959 and, for four years, Hall drove this model in no less than 22 events. Later he turned his attention to the Maserati Tipo 61 Birdcage that he raced very successfully. In 1961, he founded the Chaparral race team and was the designer of their innovative cars. He retired from the driver's seat and lives today in Midland, Texas.

Lloyd Ruby

Born in 1928 in Texas, Lloyd Ruby's racing career spun from sports cars to Indy cars spread over four decades, starting in 1957 in a Maserati 150S. From 1958 on, he successfully drove the 300S and 450S of Ebb Rose and was one of the drivers who could really handle the monster. Later Ruby raced the Lotus of 450S-owner Frank Harrison. Then he continued with Ford MK II and IV and became very active racing the Indy 500 but although he often in the lead there, he never won. He died in Texas in 2009.

Chuck Daigh

Chuck Daigh was born in California in 1923. He started road racing in the mid-1950s, campaigning a modified Mercury-Kurtis 500S. After Lance Reventlow founded his Scarab team, Daigh became his number one driver. Besides his big talent as a race driver, he was also a skilled mechanic. In the late 1950s, he drove a 450S in various races and later joined the Camoradi race team for their entry in Le Mans in 1960. He crashed in a Scarab F1 car in the British Empire Trophy in 1961, and later raced one of the Chaparrals in Sebring for Jim Hall. He died in 2008.

Tony Parravano

Born in June 1917 near Naples, Italy, Tony Parravano immigrated to the USA after World War II where he became successful in the construction business in California. His friend Tony McAfee got him interested in motorsport and he financed a Cadillac for McAfee to drive in the 1950 Carrera Panamericana. In 1951 he purchased his first Ferrari for his own "Scuderia Parravano". He hired drivers like Carroll Shelby, Phil Hill, Masten Gregory and Ken Miles and his team became quite successful. Parravano's wealth made it possible to buy more and more fast Italian sports cars. He contacted Maserati in Modena and ordered an A6GCS, a 150S, a 300S, a 350S, a 250F and two of their new 4.2-liter V8-engines for an Indianapolis project. Then he wanted a stronger motor with a car that could beat everything. It is rumored that he transferred no less than US$500,000 to Maserati which financed its 450S project. So, he became a kind of investor for Maserati and the first 450S that was built was his.

But his luck came to an end when the IRS, the US-tax authority, started to investigate his businesses. Tony Parravano disappeared in April 1960 and was never seen again. Without him, the 450S would never have existed.

Frank Harrison

Frank Harrison was the only person who owned as many as three 450S. Born in Chattanooga, Tennessee, in 1929 he was a member of a family who owned a big bottling franchise in Greensboro, North Carolina, and therefore was connected with Coca Cola. Harrison was an enthusiastic amateur driver. In March 1957 when he witnessed the impressive win by Fangio and Behra in the factory 450S at Sebring, the young industrialist was smitten and wanted such a car. Finally, he ordered one via Carroll Shelby's dealership in Dallas. He entered his new 450S in various races in the US. In September 1959, Harrison bought the used 450S from Ebb Rose, and in April 1961 he acquired the ex-Temple Buell car. Later he also became the owner of two Maserati Tipo 61 "Birdcages." Frank Harrison died in 2002.

Joe Landaker

Born in 1911, Joe Landaker became a mechanic in the US Navy. In the early 1950s he was working for the hot-tempered Tony Parravano on his Maserati and Ferrari race cars for the drivers Carroll Shelby and Masten Gregory. He later moved with Shelby to John Edgar's team. Landaker's tremendous skills as a race mechanic made him famous in the USA during the 1950s. He became the backbone of the Edgar team and was also famous for driving the GMC truck and trailer full of race cars all the way from Los Angeles to the Atlantic coast, 3,000 miles, seldom dropping under 100 mph, living on snacks and soda, and never once stopping to sleep. Coast to coast, it took him only two days.

Landaker, a modest man about his talents as a master mechanic, died in 1995.

ACKNOWLEDGMENTS

While working on this book we have to thank so many people for their collaboration and support. Their understanding, enthusiasm and almost endless patience in answering our questions and searching in their archives and collections made this book possible.

CREDITS:

Michel Bollée
Dr. Thomas Bscher
Paul-Henri Cahier
Fabio Collina
Ermanno Cozza
Will Edgar
Joel Finn †
Steve Hart
Hartmut Ibing
Mark Ketchum †
Bill Krause
Franco Lombardi
Howard Mireanu
Sir Stirling Moss †
Terry O'Neil
Willem Oosthoek
Christophe Pund
Dyke Ridgley
Napoleão Ribeiro
Peter Sachs
Jean-Marc Teissedre
Marc Vargas

…and many photographs from our own archives.

PUBLICATIONS:

AMERICAN SPORTSCAR RACING by Michael T. Lynch, William Edgar and Ron Parravano
CARIBBEAN CAPERS by Joel Finn
MASRATI 300S Vol. 1 and 2 by Walter Bäumer
MASERATI 450S by Willem Oosthoek and Michel Bollée
SPORTS CAR RACING IN THE SOUTH Vol. 1 and 2 by Willem Oosthoek
MASERATI SPORT & PROTOTYPES 1954-1965 by Michel Bollée

MASERATI: A HISTORY by Anthony Pritchard
MASERATI: THE POSTWAR SPORTS RACING CARS by Joel Finn
LA MASERATI DI ADOLFO ORSI by Nunzia Manicardi
SECOND BOOK OF MOTOR SPORT by Stirling Moss
RED HOT RIVALS by Karl Ludvigsen
THE THRILL OF THE CHASE by Colin Crabbe
SHELBY, THE RACE DRIVER by Art Evans
MASERATI IN THE WORLD SPORTS & MANUFACTURERS CHAMPIONSHIP FROM 1953 TO 1966 by Michel Bollée and Jean-François Blachette

MAGAZINES AND NEWSPAPERS:

MCA Racing News
MotoRacing
Competition Press
Speed Age
Road and Track
Auto, Motor und Sport
Jornal dos Sport
The Los Angeles Times
Car and Driver
Motor Sport
Motor Racing
Sports Car
Octane
L'Automobile
TRIDENT
AUTO ITALIANA

INTERNET SITES:

Wsrp. cz
BANDEIRA QUADRICULADA by Paulo Roberto Peralta

INDEX

MASERATI 450S CHASSIS NUMBERS

4203 289

4501 10, 30, 56, 60, 61, 62, 63, 82, 148, 188, 260, 279

4502 26, 47, 64, 65, 67, 70, 71, 72, 74, 76, 78, 79, 80, 81, 130, 132, 214, 222, 292, 293

4503 10, 17, 23, 37, 40, 62, 82, 85, 87, 88, 90, 93, 94, 96, 99, 100, 101, 102, 104, 107, 108, 110, 113, 117, 118, 119, 120, 134, 147, 148, 176, 180, 190, 260, 270

4504 10, 11, 74, 120, 121, 122, 124, 126, 127, 129, 130, 132, 133, 158, 214

4505 10, 26, 28, 37, 38, 94, 100, 132, 134, 136, 139, 141, 142, 147, 148, 174, 260

4506 42, 43, 45, 50, 132, 134, 147, 148, 151, 153, 154, 156, 158, 161, 162, 165, 166, 168, 170, 171, 172, 174, 175, 192, 196, 222, 231, 260, 292

4507 10, 26, 40, 54, 117, 118, 176, 177, 178, 180, 183, 184, 185, 187, 188, 189, 190, 191, 192

4508 10, 40, 50, 52, 53, 70, 71, 74, 118, 120, 132, 158, 192, 193, 194, 196, 198, 200, 204, 206, 209, 210, 213, 214, 218, 220, 221, 231, 237, 238, 240, 278

4509 74, 132, 214, 218, 220, 222, 223, 225, 227, 228, 231, 234, 236, 238, 239

4510 26, 45, 220, 238, 240, 242, 244, 246, 248, 251, 253, 256, 258, 259

4512 62, 117, 148, 260, 261, 266, 268, 270, 272, 273, 274, 276, 278, 279

PROPER NAMES

TRACK/RACE HISTORY BY CHASSIS

1,000 km Buenos Aires

4503   1957   20 Jan.   Juan Manuel Fangio/Stirling Moss

1,000 km Daytona, Florida

4509   1959   05 April   Lloyd Ruby/Bill Krause/Carroll Shelby

1,000 Km Nürburgring

4505   1957   26 May   Juan Manuel Fangio/Stirling Moss

12 Hours of Sebring, Florida

4503   1957   23 March   Juan Manuel Fangio/Jean Behra

1st Fall Roundup, Ft. Worth, Texas

4509   1958   12 Oct.   Ebb Rose

24 Hours of Le Mans

4503   1957   22 June   Jean Behra/André Simon

4512 (as 4501)   1957   22-23 June   Stirling Moss/Harry Schell

2nd Gran Carrera Lafitte races, Galveston, Texas

4509   1958   20 April   Ebb Rose

500 km Interlagos

4507   1961   07 Sept.   Emílio Zambello/Celso Lara Barberis/
                            Ruggero Peruzzo

Cal Club race, Riverside, California

4502   1962   03 March   Chuck Kessinger

4502   1962   04 March   Chuck Kessinger

Carrera del Alamo, San Marcos, Texas

4508   1960   17 April   Jim Hall

Chester, South Carolina

4510   1958   16 May   Dan Clippenger

Club race, Pomona, California

4502   1961   12 March   Chuck Kessinger

Coffeyville, Kansas

4510   1959   31 May   Jim Hall

Consolation race, Riverside, California

4502   1961   15 Oct.   Chuck Kessinger

4508   1960   03 April   Jim Hall

Consolation race, Times GP, Riverside, California

4502   1960   16 Oct.   Chuck Kessinger

Continental Divide Raceways, Colorado

4508   1960   16 July   Jim Hall

4508   1960   17 July   Jim Hall

Courtland, Alabama

4508   1961   02 July   Bill Kimberly

4509   1963   08-09 June   Wick Williams

4509   1963   06 July   Wick Williams

4510   1958   31 Aug.   Walt Cline

4510   1959   11 Oct.   Jim Hall

4510   1958   31 Aug.   Walt Cline

4510   1959   11 Oct.   Jim Hall

Cuba GP, Havana

4504   1958   24 Feb.   Jim Kimberly

4506   1958   24 Feb.   Carroll Shelby

4508   1958   24 Feb.   Maurice Trintignant

Danville, Virginia

4504   1958   05 Oct.   John Haas

4506   1957   04 Aug.   Carroll Shelby

Daytona, Florida

4506   1959   05 April   Jim Rathmann/Chuck Daigh

Dothan, Alabama

4510   1958   25 Oct.   Walt Cline

4510   1959   24 Oct.   Jim Hall

4510   1959   25 Oct.   Jim Hall

4510   1958   26 Oct.   Walt Cline

4510   1959   25 Oct.   Jim Hall

Examiner GP, Pomona, California

4504   1959   08 March   Hal Ullrich

4507   1962   25 May   Emílio Zambello

4508   1960   03 April   Jim Hall

4509   1959   08 March   Ebb Rose

4509   1959   07 March   Ebb Rose

4509   1960   03 April   Lloyd Ruby

Frostbite Races, Fort Worth, Texas

4504	1959	15 Feb.	Hal Ullrich

Ft. Worth, Texas

4509	1958	08 June	Ebb Rose
4510	1958	7/8 June	Dan Clippenger

Galveston, Texas

4508	1960	03 July	Jim Hall

Governor's Trophy, Nassau, Bahamas

4504	1958	05 Dec.	Ed Crawford
4506	1957	06 Dec.	Carroll Shelby
4508	1957	06 Dec.	Masten Gregory
4508	1957	08 Dec.	Masten Gregory
4508	1958	05 Dec.	Carroll Shelby
4508	1959	04 Dec.	Carroll Shelby
4510	1959	04 Dec.	Jim Hall

Hammond, Louisiana

4509	1958	30 Nov.	Ebb Rose

Hoosier GP/Indianapolis, Indiana

4508	1961	25 June	Lloyd Ruby

II Premio Anniversario, Interlagos

4507	1963	30 June	Ciro Cayres

Indy 500, Indianapolis, Indiana

4203	195	30 May	Ralph Liguori

Intl. Trophy, Nassau, Bahamas

4506	1957	08 Dec.	Carroll Shelby
4506	1958	07 Dec.	Jim Rathmann

Kiwanis GP, Riverside, California

4502	1959	19 July	Bill Krause/Pete Woods
4506	1959	19 July	Chuck Daigh
4509	1959	19 July	Lloyd Ruby

La Junta, Colorado

4508	1958	31 May	Dabney Collins

Lime Rock, Connecticut

4506	1957	28 July	Carroll Shelby
4509	1959	06 June	Lloyd Ruby

Los Angeles Examiner GP, Pomona, California

4502	1959	08 March	Bill Krause
4508	1959	08 March	Carroll Shelby

Mansfield, Louisiana

4508	1961	11 March	Jim Hall
4508	1960	06 March	Jim Hall

Meadowdale, Illinois

4509	1959	31 May	Lloyd Ruby
4509	1959	05 July	Lloyd Ruby
4509	1959	06 Sept.	Lloyd Ruby

Memorial Trophy, Nassau, Bahamas

4504	1958	07 Dec.	Ed Crawford

Miami, Florida, Orange Bowl

4508	1958	11 Jan.	Carroll Shelby
4508	1958	12 Jan.	Carroll Shelby

Mille Miglia

4501	1956	29 April	Stirling Moss/Denis Jenkinson
4503	1957	11 May	Jean Behra, DNS, crashed in testing
4505	1957	11 May	Stirling Moss/Denis Jenkinson

Montgomery, New York

4506	1957	18 Aug.	Carroll Shelby

Nassau Trophy, Nassau, Bahamas

4504	1958	07 Dec.	Ed Crawford
4508	1957	06 Dec.	Masten Gregory
4508	1958	07 Dec.	Carroll Shelby
4508	1959	04 Dec.	Lloyd Ruby
4509	1959	06 Dec.	Lloyd Ruby
4510	1959	06 Dec.	Jim Hall

Nürburgring 1,000 kms

4503	1957	26 May	Harry Schell/Hans Herrmann/Juan Manuel Fangio/Stirling Moss

A great photo of Carroll Shelby gunning through turn 3 at Pomona in March 1959. *(Walter Bäumer)*

Palm Springs, California

4506	1957	03 Nov.	Carroll Shelby
4508	1958	02 Nov.	Carroll Shelby
4508	1960	24 Jan.	Jim Hall
4508	1960	23 Jan.	Jim Hall
4506	1958	12 April	Carroll Shelby

Pomona, California

4502	1959	31 Jan.	Bill Krause
4502	1959	01 Feb.	Bill Krause
4502	1959	07 March	Bill Krause
4504	1959	07 March	Hal Ullrich
4508	1959	07 March	Carroll Shelby

Premio Rogé Fereira, Interlagos

4507	1964	08 March	Ciro Cayres

Press parade, Riverside, California

4502	1957	19 June	Dan Gurney

Race of the Two Worlds, Monza

4503	1957	30 June	Jean Behra

Rio de Janeiro GP

4507	1960	06 Nov.	Henrique Casini

Riverside, California

4506	1957	21 Sept.	Carroll Shelby
4506	1957	17 Nov.	Carroll Shelby
4506	1958	29 June	Pete Woods
4508	1957	16 Nov.	Masten Gregory

Road America, Elkhart Lake, Wisconsin

4509	1960	31 July	Lloyd Ruby
4510	1960	11 Sept.	Jim Hall/Jim Jeffords
4504	1957	23 June	Jim Kimberly

Santa Barbara, California

4502	1959	05 Sept.	Bill Krause
4502	1959	06 Sept.	Bill Krause
4506	1959	06 Sept.	Chuck Daigh

Stuttgart, Arkansas

4508	1959	18-19 April	Jim Hall

Swedish GP, Kristianstad

4501	1956	12 Aug.	Practice with Stirling Moss, Harry Schell, Piero Taruffi
4503	1957	11 Aug.	Stirling Moss/Harry Schell
4507	1957	11 Aug.	Stirling Moss/Jean Behra

Times GP, Riverside, California

4506	1958	12 Oct.	Jim Rathmann
4506	1959	11 Oct.	Chuck Daigh
4508	1958	12 Oct.	Carroll Shelby
4508	1960	16 Oct.	Jim Hall
4509	1959	11 Oct.	Lloyd Ruby

Torneio Sul-Americano, Interlagos

4507	1961	15 Jan.	Ruggero Peruzzo

Tourist Trophy, Nassau, Bahamas

4508	1957	01 Dec.	Masten Gregory

Tracy, California

4506	1958	11 May	Dan Gurney

Trophy of Two Worlds, Monza

4203	1958	29 June	Stirling Moss

Venezuela GP, Caracas

4503	1957	03 Nov.	Jean Behra/Stirling Moss/Harry Schell
4507	1957	03 Nov.	Stirling Moss/Tony Brooks
4508	1957	03 Nov.	Masten Gregory/Dale Duncan

Walterboro, South Carolina

4504	1958	04 July	Harry Rollings
4504	1958	05 July	Harry Rollings

Willow Springs test day

4502	1957	06 Jan.	Bob Drake/Jack McAfee/Richie Ginther/Dan Gurney

It was a happy day for Maserati when Behra driving #4507 crossed the finish line in Sweden 1957. *(Bilder I Syd)*

Design:	Klaus Kaminski and Walter Bäumer
Printer:	Interpress Ltd., Hungary
Page Size:	295 mm x 290 mm
Font:	Futura 9.5 pt
Text paper:	150 gsm Magno gloss
End papers:	170 gsm white woodfree offset
Dust jacket:	150 gsm glossy artpaper